Why
Meech Failed

*Lessons for
Canadian Constitutionmaking*

Raymond Breton

Observation no. 35

C.D. Howe Institute

C.D. Howe Institute publications are available from:

Renouf Publishing Company Limited, 1294 Algoma Road,
Ottawa, Ontario K1B 3W8; phone (613) 741-4333; fax (613) 741-5439

and from Renouf's stores at:

61 Sparks Street, Ottawa (613) 238-8985
211 Yonge Street, Toronto (416) 363-3171

For trade book orders, please contact:

McGraw-Hill Ryerson Limited, 300 Water Street,
Whitby, Ontario L1N 9B6; phone (416) 430-5050

Institute publications are also available in microform from:

Micromedia Limited, 165 Hôtel de Ville, Place du Portage, Phase II,
Hull, Quebec J8X 3X2

This book is printed on recycled, acid-free paper.

Canadian Cataloguing in Publication Data

Breton, Raymond, 1931–
    Why Meech failed

(Observation, ISSN 0826-9947 ; no. 35)
Includes bibliographical references.
ISBN 0-88806-305-9

1. Meech Lake Constitutional Accord (1987). 2. Canada –
Constitutional law – Amendments. 3. Canada – Politics and
government – 1984–   .* 4. Canada – Social conditions – 1971–   .*
I. C.D. Howe Institute. II. Title. III. Series: Observation
(C.D. Howe Institute). English ; no. 35.

JL65 1992.B7 1992   342.71′03   C92-093944-9

Contents

Foreword v

Acknowledgments vii

Summary ix

Chapter 1:
Symbols in Constitutional Change 1
Policy as Instrumental and Symbolic 2
Symbolic Conflicts 5
Meech Lake and Symbolic Conflict 10
Conclusion 18

Chapter 2:
Constitutional Change as a Political Process 26
Sociopolitical Causes of Confrontation 26
The Accord: An Occasion for Political Action .33
Conclusion 38

Chapter 3:
Change and Intergroup Conflict 44
Factors underlying Social Polarization 44
Outcomes of Polarization 53
Conclusion 54

Chapter 4:
The Failure to Reconcile the Irreconcilable 57
Contradictions in Canadian Society 57
Dealing with the Contradictions 67

Chapter 5:
What Did We Learn from the Meech Lake Process? 72

Bibliography 77

Members of the C.D. Howe Institute 81

Foreword

Looking back is sometimes the best way to prepare for moving forward. Certainly, as Canadians brace for the final stages of the newest round of constitutional negotiations, they should be mindful of what went wrong during the last attempt at constitutionmaking.

The Meech Lake Accord, unveiled to the country in April 1987, initially received all-party approval in the House of Commons and the backing of ten premiers. But as the June 1990 ratification deadline approached, it unraveled at an increasing pace. Last-minute attempts to save the accord were regarded with cynicism and anger by opponents; its demise sowed bitterness among proponents and, among francophone Quebecers, a sense of rejection.

To help make sense of what went wrong, the C.D. Howe Institute turned to eminent sociologist Raymond Breton of the University of Toronto. His detailed and insightful analysis of why Meech failed may serve to provide Canadians with important lessons about the pitfalls to avoid in the current round of constitutional negotiations.

The study was edited by Robert Chodos and prepared for publication by Barry A. Norris. As with all C.D. Howe Institute publications, the analysis and views presented here are the responsibility of the author and do not necessarily reflect the opinions of the Institute's members or Board of Directors.

Thomas E. Kierans
President and
Chief Executive Officer

Acknowledgments

I wish to thank Tom Kierans, Jeffrey Reitz, Gilles Houle, and Robert Chodos for their very helpful comments and suggestions on an earlier draft of this document.

I also wish to express my appreciation to David Brown, Angela Ferrante, Pierre Fortin, Irene Ip, John McCallum, Bill Robson, Daniel Schwanen, and Richard Simeon for their contributions on the occasion of a seminar on this study.

Raymond Breton
Toronto, March 1992

Summary

Canada's current exercise in changing the Constitution is reaching a critical stage. Decisions made during 1992 could be fundamental for the future of Canada. It is time to look back at the last attempt at constitutional change, the Meech Lake Accord, to understand why it failed and see what lessons can be drawn from it for the current round.

In the Meech Lake episode, the political authorities failed to take due account of the risks inherent in constitutionmaking in the Canadian context and to adopt strategies to minimize those risks. The risks relate to several aspects of constitutional change: symbolism and ambiguity; the political process; spiraling conflict; and inherent contradictions.

Symbols and Ambiguity

Background

Symbols used to confer group status in society may generate envy and tension, particularly if there is a history of competition for prestige and official status among linguistic, ethnic, or regional groups.

Since the 1982 adoption of the Charter of Rights and Freedoms, the Constitution has become a statement charged with symbolism and one to which Canadians look for an expression of their identity as a people. With the "distinct society" clause, a statement that was both highly symbolic and ambiguous, the Meech Lake Accord enlarged the symbolic component of the Constitution and multiplied the attendant risks.

It was clear to most Canadians that the distinct society clause was more than a statement of the existing order — it was a proposal for change. But the absence of a compelling explanation and justification for the change generated considerable suspicion and anxiety.

Lessons

- If symbolic statements have ambiguous implications for the distribution of power, an accompanying statement needs to clarify these implications. Legal opinions are not sufficient.
- The implications of symbolic statements for various groups need to be assessed beforehand, including historical and political factors. If they are not, those groups will naturally take that task upon themselves.
- Any symbol embedded in the Constitution that underscores ethnic, linguistic, or regional differences must be based on widespread consensus about the contexts in which such differences should be acknowledged.
- Symbols that allocate recognition or status should be balanced among the different sectors of the population. Commonality and interdependence should also be emphasized.
- If the use of symbols is unmanageable for historical or socio-political reasons, it is best to avoid them in the Constitution altogether. Recognition may be achieved through other symbolic as well as practical means.
- Although the distinct society statement has acquired such negative connotations, dropping the clause would create yet more tension, as it now has even greater significance in Quebec than it had before the Meech debate.

The Political Process

Background

For institutional change to be considered legitimate, it is not enough simply to pass it through all the legally required steps and procedures. As the Meech Lake crisis deepened, it became clear that it was not only the content of the accord that was problematic but also the political process itself. The accord's lack of legitimacy was due to several aspects of that process.

The Meech Lake Accord was presented as final. Citizens were told that they could debate the accord if they wanted to, but it would not be changed in any way. Reasons for the proposed changes were not made clear: it was simply stressed that it was urgent that they be accepted. In addition, the setting of minimum conditions suggested a refusal to compromise. The entire procedure conveyed the message that opposing views were not worth considering.

Although political elites may have had confidence in their proposal when it was initially put forward, once challenged they were at a loss. The view that political leaders lacked vision and purpose gained prominence. Increasing disagreement among the politicians themselves also hastened the loss of the public's confidence in their leaders.

Lessons

- Some government leaders and analysts see Confederation — and thus constitutionmaking — as a pact between governments, not between peoples or societies. This may have once been an accepted view, but the Meech Lake episode clearly showed that it is no longer socially valid.
- The public has a right to be presented with clearly reasoned justifications for proposed constitutional changes.
- The setting of minimum conditions should be avoided, as it is equivalent to declaring that one's victory must be total and is thus a war-cry.
- Procedures established for the discussion and adoption of proposals must contain channels for the expression of dissent.
- No matter how constitutional proposals are to be legally ratified, public discussion and informal bargaining among social groups must be recognized as essential to the process of social legitimation.
- In segmented societies such as Canada, the elites of the various segments must be committed to assuming responsibility for the whole country, not just for particular group interests, the electoral fate of their parties, and the pursuit of political power.

Spiraling Conflict

Background

In contrast to the instrumental elements of constitutions, elements that confer recognition or status — such as the distinct society clause — are not easily negotiable. Singling out a group or province in the Constitution inevitably leads others to examine what it implies for them in terms of status, power, or economic benefits. Competition and envy increase, and the ensuing tensions can damage society's cohesion and political stability.

Once a controversy is under way, an insidious process comes into play: extremists drive out those prepared to compromise, and moderates progressively disappear from the political scene. Less restrained leaders attempt to mobilize support, and more aggressive organizations arise to replace the milder, more constrained ones. As American sociologist James Coleman puts it, "Derogatory and scurrilous charges replace dispassionate issues, antagonism replaces disagreement, and a drive to ruin the opponent takes the place of the initial will to win."

In the Meech debate, politicians added to the conflict by using emotionally loaded language, thus legitimating its use by others. Rational, issue-related arguments were replaced by *ad hominem* attacks. Once people started labeling and accusing one another, the process escalated on its own, as each assertion triggered a response. By giving prominence to combative statements and fanatical acts, the media too caused extreme views to be taken as representing a whole group.

Lessons

• Political authorities must watch what they say. An argument that seems appropriate and even persuasive in the short term could have negative long-term effects. A few words can evoke latent antagonisms that threaten to change the whole climate of the debate.

- Using emotionally loaded language to convince opponents of the value of these proposals will provoke retaliation in kind, and conflict will escalate again.

Inherent Contradictions in Canadian Society

Background

Canadian society contains many sources of contradictions and, therefore, of possible social and political tensions — components of social reality that may require more or less contradictory courses of action and demands on society's resources. Aboriginality, ethnocultural pluralism, and linguistic dualism may have contradictory institutional implications. Social groups vie for rights. Regions, provinces, and nations are realities that may imply different institutional arrangements. Autonomy and interdependence, sovereignty and association, centralization and decentralization are also sources of possible contradictions when it comes to practical arrangements. The formal political equality of provinces is at odds with demographic and economic disparities. There is possible tension between collective and individual rights.

    These sources of contradictions and tensions are an intrinsic part of a richly diversified society. They may remain latent for extended periods, but various circumstances can bring them to the surface. They can be occasions of constructive change or, if exploited by political groups, they can seriously threaten the cohesion of society.

Lessons

- The idea that, somehow, contradictions can and must be eliminated for society to be better integrated and function more effectively is a myth, even though it is part of the rhetoric used by some politicians and group leaders.

- Although a society's stress threshold is impossible to measure in any systematic way, it is a vital function of leadership to judge that limit before introducing major changes.
- The legitimation of institutional arrangements, policies, and programs must be sectoral. They must be founded on basic values, but they must also take into account the particularities of different institutional sectors, segments of the society, and sociohistorical contexts.
- The purpose of a constitution is to provide a framework within which specific arrangements and policies can be negotiated while accommodating the contradictions built into particular situations. It is not an appropriate tool for regular sociopolitical bargaining in a complex, heterogeneous, federal society.
- The Constitution also needs to be stable. If it becomes an object of regular political bargaining, it will lose its nationbuilding potential and fall into the politics of interest. Instead, the Constitution should be in the politics of issues that transcend particular interests. This is clearly the case with its symbolic dimension. Also, by providing a stable framework within which practical problems can be dealt with, it can give legitimacy to the institutional system and contribute to social cohesion. This does not mean it should never be modified, but decisions to initiate constitutional changes must be based on rigorous criteria.

Chapter 1

Symbols in Constitutional Change

Almost any object, statement, document, historical fact, or monument can become a symbol for a group or society. It can come to represent something beyond its immediate reality or its practical use. Symbols are conveyors of meanings. They serve as vehicles for concepts, ideals, worldviews, and collective identities,[1] and as such can become sources of conflict. At the heart of the conflict is not the object or document itself but the concepts or ideals that it represents. Such a conflict may be over competing views of the sociopolitical order in a society, the relations among groups in that order, the proper role of particular institutions in society, and so on. In short, symbolic conflicts are struggles over different theories of society.

The context of a symbolic project, the way symbolic change is managed, and the symbolic content itself are all potentially controversial. The drafting of a constitution is full of potential for symbolic gain and loss — that is, gain and loss with regard to whose social theory should prevail in the structure of society.

But before we examine the element of symbolic conflict in the Meech Lake controversy, it is worthwhile to look briefly at the distinction between the symbolic and the legal-instrumental elements of constitutions, and of public policies more generally.[2]

---

1 See Clifford Geertz, *The Interpretation of Cultures* (New York: Basic Books, 1973).

2 See Raymond Breton, "Policy Decisions and the Competition for Symbolic Resources," in Albert Breton et al., eds., *The Competitive State* (Dordrecht: Kluwer Academic Publishers, 1991), pp. 97–112.

Policy as
Instrumental and Symbolic

Constitutions — and all policies, for that matter — usually contain a mixture of instrumental and symbolic elements, although the mix can vary considerably. Policy may deal with the structure of government, its administrative apparatus, the division of powers, the management of the economy, and the maintenance of order in society. The debate surrounding these matters tends to focus on practical implementation and on issues of effectiveness and efficiency. Institutional arrangements lend themselves well to negotiations: they can be broken down into separate, practical elements over which the give-and-take of bargaining can occur.

But these arrangements always incorporate some of the basic principles and values of a society. As such, they have a symbolic dimension: they represent the philosophy on which the social order is based, and may even be accompanied by statements to that effect. For example, policies dealing with privatization may refer to values regarded as important in a free enterprise society. Policies on the redistribution of wealth may evoke principles of justice and compassion. These references to basic principles will be convincing only if people can see the connection between the values evoked and the policy proposal and if they do not see the proposal as contradicting other important values.

Some components of a constitution or a policy are primarily symbolic and cultural, such as those dealing with identity, religion, ethics, and culture. Although they may have the practical purpose of regulating behavior or allocating resources, they are primarily affirmations of particular values in society. They signify principles of social and political organization and cultural identity, and refer to the history and projected future of the collectivity.

The underlying logic behind statements about the character of society and its values is primarily sociocultural, rather than a logic of means and ends.[3] Bargaining is thus problematic, as values and

---

3 See Kenneth A. Thompson, "Religious Organizations: The Cultural Perspective,"
   in Graeme Salaman and Kenneth Thompson, eds., *People and Organizations* (New...

principles of social order cannot easily be divided into exchangeable elements.

A policy or constitutional statement may be seen as symbolically appropriate if, for example, it expresses the society's unity, or if it conforms with certain moral values. Such a statement can affirm the importance of institutions for the maintenance of the moral order and the containment of crime, or proclaim the right to a minimum of well-being, protection against physical attack, and assistance in the event of a personal calamity.[4]

Policy and constitutional statements may also symbolically affirm the principles that ought to prevail in relations among groups in society or between groups and particular institutions — especially institutions of the state. Finally, they may give recognition to particular groups on the basis of their historical importance, their culture, or their special need for protection.

Policy and constitutional statements may also be found lacking in one or more of these respects. They can, implicitly or explicitly, rank social groups or communities by assigning to each a different status in society's central institutions. Differential allocation of status or recognition among groups may be perceived as violating basic values or as diminishing the social importance and historical role of some groups compared with others.

Questions of this sort are particularly important in a highly differentiated society such as Canada's, one that places a high premium on the equal treatment of all individuals and categories of citizens. Ideally, the symbolic statements considered legitimate in our society are those that affirm the equality of all groups or social categories.

Note 3 - cont'd.

...York: Open University Press, 1973), pp. 293–302; and idem, "Organizations as Constructors of Social Reality," in Graeme Salaman and Kenneth Thompson, eds., *Control and Ideology in Organizations* (Cambridge, Mass.: M.I.T. Press, 1980), pp. 216–236.

4 See Orrin E. Clapp, *The Collective Search for Identity* (New York: Rinehart & Winston, 1969), pp. 120–121.

In Canada, equality is generally recognized at the level of three social entities: equality of individuals, equality of provinces, and equality of the two major linguistic communities.[5] The demand of native peoples for equal status — as nations or as a province — is also rapidly gaining recognition.[6]

Words or statements that become symbols of high or low status for a province, a linguistic, ethnic, or racial group, a gender, or a religious group are likely to be resented by those who see themselves as symbolically diminished, treated as unequal, or not given due recognition. For example, the expression "founding peoples" can be very offensive to people who feel that it ignores or minimizes their own contribution to the construction of the country or who, through historical accident, are necessarily disadvantaged by this kind of distinction. Our language still contains expressions that symbolize the inferior status of women. Another example is "Parisian French," a term that symbolizes the high status of that kind of French and hence of those speaking it and the correspondingly low status of other forms of French. "Ethnic group" or "ethnics," "immigrant group" — referring to groups that have been in Canada for three or more generations — "Negro" and "Indian" are other examples of terms that symbolize an unequal status and are felt as socially denigrating by many of those so labeled.

In short, people are likely to assess not only the pragmatic-instrumental dimension but also the symbolic appropriateness of policy and constitutional statements. In fact, people may react primarily to the symbolic component of a policy or a constitution and entirely ignore its legal-instrumental dimension. Thus, there may be a strong response to a policy even if people know little about its specific technical, legal, and administrative content. Such reactions are emotional, but emotions are involved even in hardheaded economic transactions. They are rational reactions to what the symbolic statements appear to imply for their society, and for their place in it.

---

5 The possible tensions among the principles underlying these different equalities are considered in Chapter 4.

6 The equality of provinces and territories does not seem to be widely accepted yet.

Policymakers can emphasize either the instrumental or the symbolic dimension of a policy. They can decide to play down its symbolic aspects and define the task as primarily technical. Or they can decide to include in their proposals significant symbolic statements that refer to what the basic character of society is or should be. They may evoke principles of relationship among groups in society. Even if such statements are not accompanied by the specifics of implementation, they may still have long-term implications for society's organization and for the place of different groups in it.

Symbolic Conflicts

Symbolic statements are not necessarily controversial. But by their very nature, symbols assume meanings beyond their manifest content. Symbols may evoke different, even contradictory, interpretations — and corresponding emotions — from different groups.

Consequently, the use of symbols, like the use of other kinds of resources, entails risk. The nature of the risk varies according to the resource used. But whatever the resource involved — financial, technological, natural, human, or symbolic — the way it is invested and managed can yield either positive or negative results. It may not only fail to bring about the desired outcome but actually bring about the opposite of what is sought.

Several factors affect the degree to which the use of symbols can provoke social conflict. Three are considered here: the degree of ambiguity wittingly or unwittingly built into the proposals, the collective memories they bring to the fore, and the occurrence of climate-creating events. When all three factors combine, symbolic conflict is bound to occur.

The Ambiguity of Symbolic Statements

Ambiguity can be introduced into a constitution or policy to lay the foundation for particular model of society, in the hope that it can be progressively institutionalized, and it can thus pave the way for future symbolic gains. It also makes policymakers highly vulnerable, however, since ambiguity can represent an opportunity for opponents or those with a different social agenda.

Ambiguity also augments the symbolic potential of an object or statement.[7] When a statement is not given a clear, specific referent, a variety of meanings can be infused into it. Its immediate, literal meaning is likely to lose relevance as attention focuses on the ideas and values that lie behind it. Moreover, unless the statement is accompanied by a clear interpretive framework, people are likely to give it meaning in relation to their own situation, experience, and ideology or that of the groups to which they belong, rather than in relation to the intended goals of the policy.

One ambiguous element of symbolic statements is that for some people they may affirm the values and character of society, while for others they reflect a different kind of society than the one they believe exists or should exist. People in the latter category will read the statement as a threat, as it seems to propose a transformation of society and its institutions.

By augmenting the symbolic potential of a statement, ambiguity also increases the weight of the symbolic baggage it is likely to carry. For those who value what it refers to, the symbol will become increasingly important, even if it had not previously been part of the symbolic repertoire of collective self-definition. Abandoning it becomes tantamount to a surrender of identity and self-respect. But for those who fear it, it comes to symbolize what is wrong with society and the way it is governed.

The Role of Collective Memories

Individuals and groups have a history. Relations among groups also have a background that may include positive experiences but may

---

7 See Murray Edelman, *Politics as Symbolic Action: Mass Arousal and Quiescence* (New York: Academic Press, 1971); and Wendy Griswold, "The Fabrication of Meaning: Literary Interpretation in the United States, Great Britain, and the West Indies," *American Journal of Sociology* 92 (1987): 1077–1117.

involve tensions and conflicts as well. Accommodations among groups may have been worked out in the midst of intense controversies and accepted reluctantly by the various groups concerned.

The relationship between Quebec and the rest of Canada, and between English- and French-speaking Canadians, has a long history characterized by intermittent conflict over a variety of issues. Some of these have had to do with the cultural-symbolic definition of society and its institutions. Several measures have been adopted to affirm the French character of Quebec society and institutions. Other measures have attempted to transform the cultural-symbolic character of federal institutions in such a way that French Canadians can identify with them and consider them as their own and not exclusively those of another cultural group. Underlying these changes has been the principle of Canada as a bilingual society.

The cultural features of institutions and their symbolic activities influence the shaping and nourishing of people's identities. The social status of their linguistic group affects their self-esteem. Members of each collectivity will therefore take a legitimate interest in the cultural character of their institutions. They will compare the treatment that their own language and culture receives with the way other groups are treated and pay regular attention to how well "they" are doing compared with "us." Each group seeks institutional control to advance its symbolic-cultural interests.

It was in this context that the Meech Lake Accord was introduced onto Canada's political agenda and that Canadians interpreted the proposed changes. Canadians saw these changes in the light of the recent history of institutional evolution and interpreted them as further symbolic gains or losses.

Climate-Creating Events

After 1987, several events contributed to creating a climate unfavorable to a reasoned debate on the complex constitutional issues involved in the Meech Lake Accord. Various groups interpreted these events as demonstrating the shortcomings or downright unfairness of the accord. Some of the attempts to prevent the success of the accord were, of course, deliberate. But other events had a sabotaging effect that was largely inadvertent.

As mentioned earlier, the significant decline in support for the accord took place in the last six months of 1988: from 52 percent in June 1988, support fell to 31 percent by January 1989. There was also a considerable increase in the proportion of people registering no opinion. Several events during those six months may account for this shift — events that influenced the way people were interpreting the accord.

One was the bill amending the *Official Languages Act* to expand bilingual services in the federal government. This bill was passed into law in July 1988 after considerable opposition, particularly from the Western provinces. It accentuated the feeling that francophones — together with other segments of Central Canada — had disproportionate power in Ottawa and that the views of Western Canadians were not being taken into account. The reaction was a mixture of anti-French feeling, a sense of the preferential treatment of the French in Ottawa, and a genuine concern about the policy of bilingualism. All these were compounded by the overall sense of Western alienation.[8]

Another set of events had to do with Quebec's Bill 178, on the language of commercial signs.[9] The legislation was intensely debated, as it did not conform to the Canadian Charter of Rights and Freedoms — or to Quebec's own Charter of Rights. Other elements in the controversy included the use of the "notwithstanding" clause to allow its adoption and the resignation of three Quebec ministers over the bill. Coming at that particular time, there is little doubt that

---

8 Reports on the language issue in *The Western Report* from April to July 1988 express these criticisms and frustrations in unambiguous terms.

9 In December 1988, the Supreme Court of Canada declared unconstitutional the provision of Quebec's Charter of the French Language — passed in 1977 by the Parti Québécois government — forbidding any language except French on commercial signs. Using the "notwithstanding" clause in the Charter of Rights and Freedoms, which allows provinces to override some of its provisions, the Quebec National Assembly passed a new version of the restriction on languages other than French, which became known as "Bill 178."

Bill 178 colored people's view of the accord. There was extensive opposition to the bill: 76 percent of Canadians opposed it and most believed it would complicate passage of the Meech Lake Accord.[10] The Quebec government did not even receive full support from its own electorate. A December 1988 poll in that province showed that 67 percent did not agree with the government's approach to the language question.

This law gave a particular meaning to the notion of "distinct society." It was generally perceived as unfair: bilingualism was imposed in the rest of Canada while unilingualism was imposed in Quebec. The prime minister declared: "I neither approve nor do I believe it meets the tests of fairness set by the Supreme Court of Canada."[11] This message was confirmed by Manitoba's decision not to ratify the accord unless Quebec changed its policies and gave public assurances that it would not use the accord to suppress minority rights. Some people hailed the premier of Manitoba as a hero for this decision.

Another influential event was the coming into effect of Bill 8 in Ontario, which increased local services for francophones. This legislation had worried people in several municipalities partly because it was to the advantage of a particular ethnic minority, partly because that minority was French, and partly because it was seen as imposing additional financial burdens on municipalities. It contributed to the wave of declarations of unilingualism in several Ontario municipalities during the fall of 1988.

Implementing these provincial laws would probably have been controversial whatever the national circumstances. But with a major national controversy in full swing, they gained significance beyond their provincial boundaries. In English-speaking Canada, Bill 178 added momentum to the protest against the distinct society clause and special measures for francophones. In Quebec, the Ontario unilingualism movement fueled the feeling of humiliation and rejection.

---

10 Allan Gregg and Michael Posner, *The Big Picture: What Canadians Think about Almost Anything* (Toronto: Macfarlane Walter & Ross, 1990), p. 44.

11 Reported in *The Globe and Mail* (Toronto), December 22, 1988.

Another climate-creating event was the federal proposal for a free trade agreement with the United States, a major issue in the federal election in the fall of 1988. The idea of greater continental economic integration, and its possible impact on the political autonomy and cultural integrity of the country, raised considerable anxiety in English-speaking Canada. Some Canadians were even concerned for the country's survival. They saw the Meech Lake Accord as emphasizing the provincial or regional dimension of Canada while the free trade agreement promoted continental linkages and corresponding crossborder institutions. Each neglected Canada itself as a distinct entity whose cohesion needed support. A number of English Canadian nationalists saw free trade supporters in Quebec as lacking sensitivity to their English Canadian compatriots' cultural anxieties and problems of cultural and political survival.

In short, events of the second half of 1988 turned many people who had been supporters of Meech Lake, or at least undecided, against the accord. Other events continued to add new meaning to the accord in 1989 and 1990. The resignation of a federal cabinet minister and the subsequent formation of the Bloc québécois constituted another climate-creating event. It confirmed the presence of pro-independence forces — of people who were working toward the breakup of the country — in the federal government. It was the symbol of an inimical force at work at the very center of power. Furthermore, events that had taken place before the accord was even negotiated, such as past measures to accommodate linguistic and ethnic groups, were reinterpreted in the context of the current debate.

Meech Lake and Symbolic Conflict

The Meech Lake proposal for constitutional change included ambiguous statements — in particular, the distinct society concept. No coherent explanation of this concept was provided, even though it was the one most subject to discussion and controversy. The Quebec government was adamant in refusing to define it. The explanations supplied by first ministers were vague and, in a number of instances, contradictory. One premier even said that he was not quite sure what the concept meant and that its meaning would eventually have to be spelled out by the courts. Little attention was given to the process of legitimation. No systematic framework was presented to explain the changes and to justify them in relation to a public philosophy. Why?

The authorities seemed to be confident either that there would be little dissent, or that if aspects of the proposal were questioned a consensus would soon spontaneously emerge. Perhaps they believed they could manage the process so that the accord would eventually be ratified. Perhaps they were at a loss as to how to legitimate the scheme, or perhaps they simply did not think about this aspect of the situation.

The distinct society clause was seen as having implications for the structuring of institutions and the division of powers. But since no framework was presented to explain what the changes would mean and why they were necessary, questions and criticisms were inevitable.

Largely because of its ambiguity, the accord raised several questions. The most important one was this: Was the accord simply an official recognition of Quebec's cultural distinctiveness, or was it a mechanism for redistributing power?

The Pursuit of Power

In English-speaking Canada, the central issue raised by the accord was one of power and, by and large, the opposition to it was based on arguments related to power. Thus, it was argued, the socio-economic condition of francophones had improved considerably during the past 30 years or so and they had made power gains both in Quebec and across the country.

Several opponents also considered that the federal distribution of power was now somewhat unbalanced in favor of Quebec and of francophones generally. They perceived Quebec as having a decisive influence over national issues and over who is elected at the federal level. For them, the accord would simply accentuate that influence and, by the same token, their own relative lack of influence. They accordingly opposed it.

This view was particularly prevalent in Western Canada — symbolized by the federal government's 1986 decision to award the maintenance contract for the Canadian Forces' CF-18 jet fighter to a Montreal company when a Winnipeg firm had submitted a lower bid. It was also present in parts of Ontario and the Atlantic provinces; its most potent symbol in Newfoundland, for example, was the unfavorable terms under which the province sells electric power from Churchill Falls to Quebec.

Of course, not all English-speaking Canadians shared that diagnosis of the situation. Many, while acknowledging that francophones had made power gains, did not consider that these gains favored francophones unfairly. Judging from the results of polls on attitudes toward official bilingualism, the changes were supported by a majority of English-speaking Canadians.[12] However, even those who did not perceive an unbalance found it difficult to justify further changes — or at least the changes proposed by the accord. While many social and intellectual leaders in English-speaking Canada came forward to defend controversial institutional changes in the 1960s and 1970s, fewer were prepared to support the accord.

This reticence may have been due to recent changes in the main orientation of English-French bargaining and accommodation. A few decades ago, there was a consensus that the grievances voiced by francophones — particularly by those in Quebec — were legitimate and that something had to be done about them. But many of those who had acknowledged such grievances now appeared to believe the changes made during the past 30 years had rectified the situation. For example, a 1991 Environics survey showed that 49 percent of a Canada-wide sample thought that, compared with other

---

12 For a review of survey results on this matter, see Canada, Office of the Commissioner of Official Languages, Policy Analysis Branch, *An Analysis of Attitudes towards Official Languages Policy among Anglophones* (Ottawa, 1990).

parts of the country, Quebec was *better off*. Among Quebecers, the corresponding percentage was almost the same, at 47 percent.[13]

People thus found it difficult to interpret the accord as a further rectification of grievances. It was easier to assess it in terms of claims for power, as expansionist rather than corrective. Some believed the political power of francophones had become disproportionate to their population, and that the French language was becoming too predominant. It was now the turn of other groups to have their grievances addressed.

The main language provided by our political culture to justify the acquisition of power is that of the rectification of socio-economic or political inequities. For instance, it was suggested that the accord was necessary because, in 1982, an injustice had been inflicted on Quebec "for which it was necessary to obtain forgiveness." Thus, the accord was "the price of Quebec's forgiveness."

But the language of grievance was not enough to convince most English-speaking Canadians, as the nature of the injustice involved was not specified. Did it refer to the process of patriation, or to the fact that existing institutional arrangements were unjust for Quebec? Or both? Many English-speaking Canadians did not see the 1982 constitutional patriation and change as an injustice toward Quebec; more pertinent to them was the fact that the negotiations were carried out on Quebec's behalf by a government dedicated to Quebec's political independence.

If the language of grievance cannot be applied, change must be justified in reference to valued objectives: that it will improve an already acceptable situation, that it represents a move toward some social or moral ideal, or that it is in line with what people understand their society to be and thus confirms elements that are already part of people's identity.

---

13 The survey used a sample of 2,012 respondents. The question was: "Would you classify each of the following regions as better off, less well-off, or about average?" Interestingly, among respondents who supported the Reform Party, 56 percent thought that Quebec was better off.

But proponents of the accord were unable to justify it in terms of a positive overall conception of Canadian society. Rather, they justified it in terms of the urgency of having it passed. The need for Quebec to be able to sign the Constitution "with honor and enthusiasm" was stressed. The importance of bringing Quebec back into the Canadian family was emphasized. These were positive justifications for ratification, but they did not begin to deal with the particular changes introduced by the accord.

Proponents also stressed the consequences of failing to ratify the accord. Such failure, they argued, would mean that, as the prime minister put it, "Quebec's isolation would become a fact of constitutional life,...slowly creating two Canadas in respect to the country's basic law."[14] It was also suggested that the accord would increase the legitimacy of federal institutions in Quebec. But the reasons the changes were necessary were not spelled out, except that they were the minimum conditions set by Quebec. In short, justification was only negative: failing to ratify the accord would have detrimental consequences.

Another dimension of the power issue was increased autonomy for Quebec. This dimension was central to the political discourse in Quebec: not more power in Ottawa, but more power in Quebec City, justified in terms of francophone Quebecers' distinctiveness and special needs as a linguistic minority in North America.

One result of the Quiet Revolution is that state institutions have replaced the Roman Catholic Church as the embodiment and locus of Quebec's identity and culture. More political autonomy is, accordingly, seen as the natural evolution of its *projet de société*, its cultural self-realization.

The reaction of English-speaking Canadians to Quebec's demands for increased autonomy was ambivalent. On the one hand, they generally recognized and accepted Quebec's distinctiveness. On the other hand, they questioned whether its locus should be the Quebec government rather than Quebec society. They also ques-

---

14 Quoted in an editorial in *The Globe and Mail* (Toronto), June 4, 1987.

tioned the underlying intentions of the quest for autonomy. Did Quebec really need more powers to protect francophones' language and culture? Or was it a disguised pursuit of sovereignty-association, through which Quebec could reap the advantages of federalism while bearing as little of the cost as possible? Quebec would then have increased its powers at the provincial level while retaining its considerable influence in federal decisions and in the allocation of national resources.

Some English Canadians suspected that the distinct society clause was a symbolic instrument introduced in the Constitution to be used later in the pursuit of more powers, and that the accord was another step in a process with no foreseeable end. Further claims would surely be forthcoming if Meech were to be ratified.

Political authorities and analysts were not able to convince the suspicious that this was not the case — that some additional autonomy was necessary, but sovereignty was not the *de facto* outcome. On the contrary, some Quebec government officials suggested that the accord was just the beginning of a substantial transfer of powers and that the distinct society clause was to be used for this purpose in subsequent negotiations. Its significance would be interpreted by the courts in the light of the new needs of Quebec society. The terms of reference of the Allaire Committee, set up about four months *before* the Meech Lake deadline, also clearly stated that the accord was only a step in preparation for subsequent negotiations. It recommended a massive transfer of powers to the province.[15]

Finally, the more cynical saw the disproportionate importance given to the public desecration of the Quebec flag in Brockville, Ontario,[16] and, more generally, the emphasis that Quebec politicians and opinionmakers placed on the themes of rejection and humiliation as ways of concealing the real nature of the clause — the creation of a constitutional instrument for the pursuit of power.

---

15 See Quebec Liberal Party, Constitutional Committee, *A Quebec Free to Choose* (Quebec, January 28, 1991). The committee's chairman was Jean Allaire.

16 This event, which took place in the fall of 1989, was subsequently shown many times on television in Quebec.

Recognition and Status

While in English-speaking Canada the accord was perceived as
dealing with power, in French-speaking Quebec the central notions
were recognition and status.[17] The questions and opposition expressed by English Canadians were perceived as a refusal to recognize Quebec's distinctiveness, both cultural and historical. They
were also considered a withdrawal of historically acquired status in
the federation.[18] Losing something is probably always more painful
than failing to acquire it.

One of the anxieties of francophone Quebecers is the fear of
being reduced to the status of other ethnic groups. Because of this
they regard the federal policy of multiculturalism with suspicion —
even though the Quebec government has adopted essentially the
same policy, albeit with another name. This status anxiety is also at
the root of Quebec's resistance to the notion of the equality of the
provinces.

A Quebec minister said in late 1991 that "Quebec will never
accept to be treated at the same level...because we are distinct first,
but also because of our population, and because of our status in the
federation."[19] Treatment at the same level would be a withdrawal of
that status.

The vocabulary used to denounce opposition to the accord and
to the distinct society clause included terms such as humiliation,
rejection, isolation, and being put in one's place. Such perceptions
were cast in the context of the history of English-French relations in
Canada. For instance, a number of francophone Quebecers believed
nothing had been done to recognize the distinctiveness of Quebec
and to accommodate its cultural and linguistic character during the

---

17 For a convincing argument that the distinction between power, on the one hand,
and acceptance and status, on the other, pervades theoretical thinking in the social
sciences, see Theodore D. Kemper and Randall Collins, "Dimensions of Micro-
interaction," *American Journal of Sociology* 96 (1990): 32–68.

18 On withdrawal of status, see Everett E. Hagen, *On the Theory of Social Change*
(Homewood, Ill.: Dorsey Press, 1962).

19 Reported in *The Globe and Mail* (Toronto), November 6, 1991.

past 30 years. The considerable institutional changes that had taken place as well as the changes in attitudes and behavior in a large segment of the anglophone population were either not known, considered irrelevant for the current debate, or dismissed as too little, too late.

Another view was that francophones could not rely on anglo-phones for their cultural survival and vitality: they had to assume the entire responsibility themselves. In fact, a common view was that English Canada had not only not helped in this regard but had offered resistance all along. For English Canadians, this view held, the experience of institutional change meant having had French "rammed down their throats."

From this perspective, English Canada's refusal to accept the distinct society clause was yet another instance of resistance to Quebec's cultural aspirations. It was an attempt to weaken or abolish existing institutional measures to protect and enhance the cultural and linguistic character of Quebec and the francophone presence in national institutions and to forestall any additional ones. The insis-tence in English Canada on the Charter of Rights and Freedoms was simply a way of disguising the opposition to those measures. The emphasis on individual rights was thus a device to oppose the collective rights of francophones; indeed, to reject the very idea that there are such things as collective rights.

Just as some francophone Quebecers made statements that confirmed the pursuit-of-power diagnosis that was widespread in English Canada, so there were expressions of rejection and humilia-tion — such as the desecration of the Quebec flag and statements by leaders of extremist groups — that confirmed the rejection-and-humiliation diagnosis that came to prevail in Quebec. The repeated showing of the Brockville flag incident on Quebec television was widely interpreted as a systematic attempt to portray English Cana-dians as vicious and to arouse feelings against them.

These diagnoses — a question of power on the one hand, a question of acceptance and respect on the other — came to dominate the interpretive schemes on each side of the linguistic divide. It was

increasingly difficult for English Canadians to see that Quebec faced
cultural problems that were quite different from those of the rest of
the country, and to consider that perhaps some special measures
were needed to cope with them. It also became very difficult for
francophone Quebecers to recognize the considerable goodwill
among anglophones and to acknowledge the magnitude of the
changes that had already taken place. They found it impossible to
believe that the grievances and frustrations of people in certain parts
of English Canada over the distribution of power in federal decisionmaking and over the power wielded by Quebec — and, one might
add, by Ontario and Toronto — perhaps had some validity and were
not simply expressions of anti-Quebec feelings.

Conclusion

This analysis of the symbolic dynamic of the Meech Lake controversy leads to suggestions for dealing with the symbolic component
of the Constitution and for finding a framework that validates
institutional change.

Dealing with the Symbolic
Component of Constitutions

Constitutional documents usually have instrumental rather than
symbolic value. This was the case, for example, with Canada's
original constitution, the *British North America Act* of 1867.[20]
     But since the 1982 patriation, the Constitution has acquired
considerable symbolic value, particularly because of its Charter of
Rights and Freedoms. For many Canadians, it does more than specify their rights as members of society. It is a statement about the
character of Canada and something with which people identify. With
the distinct society clause, a statement that was almost exclusively

---

20 Northrop Frye wrote that "the main thing wrong with Confederation was its
   impoverished cultural basis" (*The Globe and Mail* [Toronto], April 15, 1991).

symbolic, the Meech Lake Accord enlarged the symbolic component of the Constitution, although, as discussed earlier, it was also thought to be an instrument for subsequent power gains.

All societies — indeed, all groups and organizations — have a symbolic repertoire through which they represent who they are as collective entities and through which they affirm and celebrate their character and values. The repertoire may include a name, a costume, a flag, a founding myth, monuments, rituals, and ceremonies whereby special historical events and heroes are celebrated. For Canada, this repertoire has come to include the Constitution.

As we have seen, symbolic policy statements are risky: their ambiguity may have a divisive rather than an integrating effect. Several statements of the "Canada Clause" included in the current constitutional proposals seem to be safe in this regard.[21] They refer to basic values over which there is a widespread consensus. In that regard, the clause might therefore have an integrating effect. On the other hand, it also contains controversial statements that may neutralize that positive effect. It is not the positive elements that will "sanctify" the controversial ones; rather, it is the controversial ones that are likely to contaminate the overall symbolic affirmation.

Symbols that allocate group status in society may generate envy and tension among those groups, particularly if there is a history of competition for prestige and official status among linguistic, ethnic, or regional groups.[22]

This does not mean that status symbols should be avoided in constitutional documents. It means that if the symbols allocate status or recognition, the distribution must be balanced among the major territories or population segments in society. The forms of recognition need not be the same for all groups or social categories, but they

---

21 See Canada, *Shaping Canada's Future Together: Proposals* (Ottawa: Supply and Services Canada, 1991), pp. 9–10.

22 On the allocation of symbolic resources, see Raymond Breton, "The Production and Allocation of Symbolic Resources: An Analysis of the Linguistic and Ethnocultural Fields in Canada," *Canadian Review of Sociology and Anthropology* 21 (1984): 123–144.

need to be balanced or they are likely to have a divisive impact.[23] Commonness and interdependence should also be symbolically emphasized. A statement that suggests special status based on anything other than achievement is likely to be rejected, unless it is legitimated in reference to stated and accepted values.[24]

In a highly differentiated society such as Canada, any symbol embedded in the Constitution that underscores ethnic, linguistic, or regional differences raises the social and political awareness of these differences and is fraught with risks for the cohesion of society. Again, this does not mean that such symbols should not be used, but they should be based on widespread consensus about the contexts in which such differences should be acknowledged.

If the use of symbols is unmanageable for historical or socio-political reasons, it is best to avoid them altogether, however meaningful they may be for a particular group. Recognition may be achieved through other symbolic as well as practical means.

Given the "unbalanced" nature of the distinct society statement and the negative connotations it acquired, it seems obvious that, for the sake of social cohesion, it would be best to drop it from the Constitution. But dropping the clause now would create still more tension because of the greater significance it has acquired in Quebec since the confrontation. However, as the central objection to the distinct society clause did not relate to a rejection of the distinctive character of Quebec but rather to its ambiguous implications for the distribution of power, the constitutional statement needs to clarify this question. Legal opinions on whether the clause gives more power to Quebec may not be sufficient, and anyway there is no legal consensus on the matter.

---

23 The suggestion by a provincial premier that all provinces be recognized as distinct societies was, at the time, dismissed out of hand. But it did contain a valuable insight — namely, that status should be allocated equally if the distribution is to have legitimacy. See also Karl W. Deutsch, "Political Community and the North Atlantic Area," in *International Political Communities: An Anthology* (Garden City, N.Y.: Anchor Books, 1966), pp. 34–35.

24 It seems, for example, that many Canadians are prepared to accept a special status for native peoples on historical grounds.

An additional statement must make it clear that recognition as a distinct society does not imply more powers for Quebec, that it would not be used in the future to obtain more powers, and that Quebec's distinctiveness would simply be recognized within existing constitutional arrangements. This may be unacceptable to Quebec, given statements by Quebec officials during the course of the controversy. However, a senior Quebec cabinet minister said in 1991 that "if Quebec wants to be recognized as distinct, it's not because we want more powers or to be considered as superior. We don't want to be better, but we do want to be legally recognized as being different."[25] If this could be taken as an official position, the proposed clarification would be acceptable to Quebec.

As noted elsewhere in this book, however, other statements by Quebec officials have indicated that power *was* one of the intentions behind the distinct society clause. The existence of different interpretations of the clause and the fact that contradictory statements were made are additional reasons for a clarification in the Constitution itself.

The underlying ideas are, first, that the vitality of a community's culture depends on the vitality of its institutions and, second, that special measures may be required to protect and strengthen these institutions, particularly in view of the predicament of a francophone minority in anglophone North America. Once the reality of this situation is recognized, several issues need to be considered.

First, what powers are needed to maintain the vitality of the cultural community? Some argue that the state must be active in all institutional spheres: political, economic, cultural, and social (this is the position of the Allaire report); others maintain that the powers involved are those concerning language and culture.

Second, to what extent is the state the main agent of cultural maintenance and development? Should there not be more reliance on civil society? In contemporary Quebec political culture, the state is paramount; civil society is assigned a relatively small role. It should be noted that this is a relatively new phenomenon: the

---

25 See Peter C. Newman, "The Closet Federalism of the Parti Québécois," *Maclean's*, December 30, 1991, p. 20.

transformation and revitalization of Quebec society in the course of
the Quiet Revolution was primarily a civil society phenomenon. The
state became active in it, but its involvement was largely the result
of a social movement. Now, change is much more under the direction
and management of the state.

But the limits of government in preserving culture need to be
recognized. Modern communication technologies have a way of
bypassing government policies, as Canada and several other coun-
tries are finding out. The massive influence of the United States
cannot be stopped at the border by a law. English as the *lingua franca*
of international relations in commerce, diplomacy, and science is a
reality beyond the scope of Canadian legislation. The cultural impact
of economic and political transactions with the rest of Canada and
with the United States cannot be removed by legal specifications or
transfers of powers. Cultural maintenance and development relies
heavily on civil society.

Third, what level of government should assume the responsibility of the institutional and cultural vitality of the francophone
population of Quebec? This is perhaps the most important issue
underlying the distinct society proposal. Generally, the view in
English-speaking Canada as well as in Quebec is that this responsibility belongs to Quebec. Some, however, feel that the federal government also has a role to play in this regard and that, in fact, it is
already assuming such a responsibility. It has contributed significantly to the Quebec economy, to its educational, health, and social
welfare institutions, to its research capability, and even to its cultural
development.[26]

The ways in which this issue is dealt with can profoundly affect
the evolution of Canadian society. The more the protection and
vitality of Quebec as a distinct society is defined as belonging to
Quebec, the less the federal government would have a meaningful
role in that province and the less would be its linkages with Quebec
residents. instead, its relationships would be with the Quebec gov-

---

26 The Canada Council, Radio-Canada, and the National Film Board are federal
   initiatives that have played a crucial role in Quebec.

ernment, not with its citizens either directly or through a variety of institutions. As a result, Quebecers' already weak identification with the federal government would become even weaker. Ottawa would be defined as a tax collector and a manager of distant functions such as defense.

The alternative would be to define the vitality of Quebec as a distinct society as a responsibility of both level of governments — a view that is not new in Canadian federalism but that would need to be rejuvenated. Of course, moving in that direction would be difficult at the moment. Indeed, Quebec's political and bureaucratic elites and intelligentsia largely reject such a view: as noted, this appears to be the force behind the constitutionalization of the notion of distinct society.

In addition, English-speaking Canada would need to accept such a responsibility. In other words, a significant way of recognizing Quebec's distinctiveness would be to accept a role in maintaining it. At the moment, this acceptance does not appear to have taken hold. A 1990 public opinion poll showed that 57 percent of English-speaking Canadians did not agree with the proposition that "in view of the dominance of English in North America, the French language needs special protection in Quebec to ensure its survival."[27] By contrast, 94 percent of francophones agreed with the statement. However, as anglophones probably interpreted the statement in the context of Bill 178 and of other recent tensions over language legislation, support might have been higher — 35 percent disagreed and 22 percent strongly disagreed — if the special measures had been seen to entail positive programs rather than restrictive laws.

The Need to Legitimate Institutional Change

In order for institutional change to take place and to be considered legitimate, it is not enough to simply pass it through all the legally

---

27 *The Globe and Mail* (Toronto), July 9, 1990.

required steps and procedures.[28] The legitimacy of a constitution depends on the extent to which people accept its basic ideas. A legitimating framework must help people make sense of the innovations by explaining the proposals, and it must justify them by showing that the values embedded in the policy are congruent with widely acceptable cultural values.

When this is the case, the statements reinforce the values and worldviews of citizens by making them explicit. The constitution becomes a monument celebrating what people consider the underpinnings of their social and political world. But if no such scheme is provided, if the link between the proposed change and an accepted system of ideas and values is not made explicit, citizens may not regard the proposed change as valid.

The absence of a compelling explanation and justification for the Meech Lake proposals generated considerable suspicion and anxiety: was the basic character of Canadian society being changed by that proposal? If so, how? This vacuum also opened the stage to active competition among different conceptions or theories of Canadian society and of its political organization. And once the competition was in full swing, articulating a legitimating framework became an almost impossible task, as arguments put forward to justify (or oppose) the proposal were perceived as self-serving.

Once the controversy was under way, the political authorities were confronted with a serious dilemma. On the one hand, what was the point of formally adopting the changes when they were not widely considered legitimate? (For those who demand social as well as legal validation of institutional change, the failure of the accord can be seen as a success.) On the other hand, once a high level of emotional and ideological fervor had been reached, it became almost impossible to withdraw the proposal without making matters even

---

28 On legitimacy and legitimation, see "The Sociology of Legitimation," *Current Sociology* 35 (1987, special issue); Paul M. Hirsch, "From Ambushes to Golden Parachutes: Corporate Takeovers as an Instance of Cultural Framing and Institutional Integration," *American Journal of Sociology* 91 (1986): 800–837; and Jeffrey Pfeffer, "Management as Symbolic Action: The Creation and maintenance of Organizational Paradigms," *Research in Organizational Behavior* 3 (1981): 1–52.

worse. A postponement of the deadline (as some were requesting) would probably have been the best course of action, since it would have made it easier to make explicit the theory of Canada underlying the proposal and to explain and justify it to the people of Canada.

Chapter 2

Constitutional Change as a Political Process

In a democracy, any public issue is fair game for political competition and promotion. Political parties and organized interest groups may see in any situation, including constitutional change, an opportunity to promote their own political agenda and make electoral headway.

In the Meech Lake episode, the debate was increasingly politicized until it became a major confrontation. While the previous chapter discussed the symbolic dynamic of this evolution, this chapter examines how political circumstances also contributed to it.

Sociopolitical Causes of Confrontation

The conditions that contributed most to the evolving confrontation were:

- the scope of the change;
- the lack of an institutional mechanism to respond to criticism;
- the strategy of minimum demands;
- the ambiguity of some provisions of the proposal;
- a lack of public confidence in the political elites; and
- the residuum of past controversies.

The Scope of the Institutional Change

The more significant the institutional change, the more likely it is to be controversial. Constitutional changes are highly significant, since they concern the basic "rules of the game" in society and may have long-lasting implications for different social groups.

The Meech Lake Accord clearly entailed a change that many, including the political authorities who negotiated the proposal, considered major. In fact, these authorities deliberately drew attention to it, lauding it as a solution to a serious societal problem and proclaiming it a great achievement.

The Lack of a Mechanism to Respond to Criticism

There was an important difference between the Meech Lake Accord and the normal process of policymaking: it was final. The proposals were not meant to be debated, revised, re-debated, and re-revised as necessary. Citizens were told that they could debate the accord if they wanted to, but that it would not be changed in any way.

The objective seems to have been to present citizens with an authoritative decision and to avoid public participation. The authorities may have feared that the proposal was so controversial that a public debate would endanger its ratification. Or perhaps, in the political culture of governing elites in Canada, this is just the way constitutional changes are made: people in positions of authority must make decisions and the population should defer to their judgment.[1] All that is needed is a well-timed and well-orchestrated public relations campaign.

But decisionmaking procedures are also communicative acts: they send messages to citizens. The message may be to reassure them that their interests will be taken into account. In this case, the procedure conveyed the message that opposing views were not worth considering or were politically irrelevant. An absence of channels through which people could express dissent violated a basic democratic value and undermined the very legitimacy of the process.

---

1 See Edgar Z. Friedenberg, *Deference to Authority: The Case of Canada* (White Plains, N.Y.: M.E. Sharpe, 1980).

Thus, the combination of a symbolic put-down and violation of a basic value generated cynicism, frustration, and anger, especially among those who felt that they had something to lose in the proposed policy.

This was one of the first signs of a change in the climate of attitudes. People's attention shifted away from the content of the agreement toward broader matters of power, status, and recognition, and toward the adequacy of the process of democratic representation in the process itself. It was not that the political authorities had taken the initiative that offended people. Indeed, people expect those in authority to draw up policy, especially when it involves complex technical matters. But people also expect to be given an opportunity to voice their concerns and interests, and they expect that the authorities will take these into account.

The Strategy of Minimum Demands

Setting minimum conditions is also likely to lead to confrontation, as its underlying message is a refusal to negotiate and compromise. It is equivalent to saying that one's victory must be total, however unacceptable some groups may find the demands.[2] This was the situation with the Meech Lake Accord. The political authorities gave no clues as to what modifications they could accept without the compromises being symbolically defined as a defeat. On the contrary, the they repeated that any change *would* be a defeat. When no alternative is available, the opposition then also defines victory as total. Hence, many critics of the accord vowed to try to defeat the whole proposal.

The political authorities claimed that compromises had already been made and were incorporated into the negotiations. This may well have been the case, but since the negotiations had been carried

---

2 On the conditions for the termination of conflicts, see Lewis A. Coser, "The Termination of Conflict," *Journal of Conflict Resolution* 5 (1961): 347–353.

out in secret, the public could not have known the extent or nature of these compromises.[3]

The Ambiguity of
Parts of the Proposal

The importance of ambiguity in defining the symbolic potential of public policies and regulations has already been discussed. The role of ambiguity, however, can be more complex. It can be deliberately introduced into a policy to give those in power an opportunity to increase their power. They can then use this built-in ambiguity, for example, to expand the range of activities under their jurisdiction.

Failure to specify the power implications of a constitutional provision — and those whom the provision is likely to advantage and disadvantage — may also increase the level of suspicion in segments of the population. Some pro-independence Quebecers interpreted the vagueness of the accord as a way of ostensibly giving something to Quebec that in fact gave nothing. On the contrary, they saw it as a smoke screen covering the power ambitions of Ottawa and the rest of Canada. On the other hand, many in English-speaking Canada saw in it a device that Quebec could later use to increase its power in the federation.

Once their opponents use the ambiguity for their own purposes, policymakers may find they have become the victims of their own power strategies.

Lack of Public
Confidence in Political Elites

Controversy can also grow when political elites do not appear to have the situation under control. They may have been confident in

---

3 On this matter, see Andrew Cohen, *A Deal Undone: The Making and Breaking of the Meech Lake Accord* (Vancouver: Douglas & McIntyre, 1990).

their proposal when it was initially put forward, but once challenged they are at a loss. The view that there was a lack of vision and purpose among political leaders may have been in part an expression of this concern.[4] Individuals and groups that appear to have a clear idea of where they are going then acquire correspondingly more influence.

A breakdown of consensus among political and social elites also causes loss of public confidence. As long as trusted authorities and social leaders present a united defense of an institutional change, and as long as their disagreements are on secondary, practical features of the proposal and not on its basic principles, the proposal is not likely to be seriously challenged. But when there is disagreement on fundamentals among elites, opponents will feel that their suspicions are confirmed. The criticism of social and political leaders conveniently provides people who are uneasy about a policy with a language in which to express their concerns.

In the case of Meech Lake, there was consensus at the federal level among the party leaders. There was also consensus among the first ministers who signed the document. But this soon changed. Provincial elections not only replaced some of those first ministers but also provided a forum for opposition parties and other groups to question the accord.

The suspicion that some political elites were biased against particular groups further depleted public confidence. The federal and Quebec governments were seen as being heavily under the influence of Quebec nationalists, including those who favored independence. Their sway was also indirect: they played such a strong role in the diffusion of information in Quebec that they could control public perceptions and attitudes. Political authorities were thus seen as *téléguidés* by proponents of sovereignty-association and independence. Many saw these groups as the principal force behind the initiation of the process of constitutional change in the first place.

---

4 See Canada, Citizen's Forum on Canada's Future [Spicer Commission], *Report* (Ottawa, 1991), pp. 96–101.

The Residuum of Past Controversies

As already indicated, collective memories are important in shaping people's perceptions and behavior. During the past 30 years or so, with the support of many English-speakers, francophones had increased their economic, political, and cultural presence in public institutions in Quebec and on the national scene. This is the process that came to be known as the Quiet Revolution.

Quebecers had changed. Higher levels of education, a changing identity, rising expectations, and power aspirations led to attempts to conquer or reconquer institutional spaces. The process meant confronting those who controlled those spaces. These included the traditional French Canadian elites, such as the clergy, some politicians, professionals, and small business. They also included the English-speaking groups dominating the Quebec economy, the politico-bureaucratic groups controlling the federal government, and the groups of neither French nor British origin who had allied themselves with the anglophones and who supported their institutions.

As noted earlier, many of the changes — and the resistance to them — were related to the symbolic-cultural character of institutions. But the agenda of the new contending groups also entailed gaining control of the means necessary for organizationbuilding, particularly political power and capital. It meant partly or completely displacing those occupying the coveted organizational space and claiming new spaces that English-speaking groups would, under the previous dispensation, have considered their own "turf."

Changes in the linguistic rules of the game were a crucial weapon used to gain additional institutional control. Although state powers had earlier been used to impose the English language in other provinces, the use of state powers to impose French was new in Quebec.

Language legislation was part of a larger strategy aimed at increasing francophone control of the Quebec economy. The legislation aimed at opening avenues of social mobility to francophones in organizations where the prevalence of English acted as a barrier for many upwardly mobile francophones. Other components of the

strategy involved taking over enterprises previously owned by anglophones, establishing state agencies for the accumulation of capital, and gaining control of sources of capital that already existed or
were being created — such as public pension funds.

Since the vitality of organizational systems, public or private,
depends partly on the population size, immigration flow was di-
rected toward French institutions. This entailed gaining greater control over the admission of immigrants, requiring that the children of
immigrants attend the French educational system, and establishing
programs for the integration of immigrants.

Other strategies were designed to integrate Quebec into the
sociopolitical fabric of the larger Canadian society. In particular, they
encouraged an increased presence of francophones in federal institutions, both political and administrative. One aim was to increase
the power of French Canadians in the definition of national goals
and in the allocation of national resources. Another was to convert
federal institutions from a largely unilingual to a bilingual system.
With the support of many anglophones, these objectives were
achieved to a significant degree.

Of course, these changes encountered resistance. Both English-
and French-speakers want to expand their organizational domain to
provide more opportunities for members of their group. Both want
institutions that embody their culture and operate in their language.
If one group organizes to exert pressure for institutional changes, the
other is likely to oppose it. Institutional change does not occur
without a serious struggle.

The past three decades have witnessed an almost continuous
process of institutional change accompanied by an almost continuous controversy between groups on the two sides of the linguistic
divide. Many accommodations have been made, but the conflicts are
still vivid in each group's collective memory. This is the "burden of
history" that must be taken into account in policymaking.[5]

---

5 See Harold Guetzkow, "Isolation and Collaboration: A Partial Theory of Inter-
   Nation Relations," *Journal of Conflict Resolution* 1 (1957): 46–68.

Frequently, there is a residuum of resentment and hostility over "losses" incurred, especially if the "winners" do not readily recognize their gains but appear to want even more. Particular incidents become symbols of this negative residuum. In Western Canada, the decision to award the CF-18 fighter maintenance contract to a Quebec firm was such a symbol. Many saw the distinct society clause as synonymous with what the CF-18 incident symbolized: the advantage enjoyed by Quebec in federal decisionmaking. The accord would accentuate this advantage and was therefore unacceptable. The mention of such incidents evoked an array of negative memories and erased positive ones.

The Accord:
An Occasion for Political Action

All the necessary ingredients for political opportunism were thus present: ambiguity ripe for exploitation, loss of confidence in authorities, disagreement among authorities and opinion leaders, and memories of past controversies.

Several groups took advantage of the opportunity. Among those were opposition parties, as is predictable in a multiparty democracy. Those with political, cultural, or economic grievances were also active participants, as were people who wanted to enter the political stage or move toward its center. Those with strong resentments against people in power, those who had strong ideological commitments to a particular cause, and those who were acutely preoccupied with what they considered an injustice or an evil all saw potential for political gain.

The opposition parties that saw their opportunity were the Parti Québécois in Quebec, the New Democratic Party in the West, and the Liberals in Manitoba. However, it was to the Parti Québécois that Meech Lake provided the greatest opportunity. The PQ was still suffering from the internal conflicts and occasional tensions between the government and the party, the defeat of the referendum on sovereignty-association in 1980, the resignation of several ministers, and its electoral defeat in 1985.

After the referendum some analysts declared that the pro-independence and ultranationalist movement in Quebec was dead. It was not dead, however, but only experiencing an organizational crisis. The PQ had succeeded in becoming almost synonymous with the nationalist cause in Quebec. If one was a strong nationalist, one tended to support the PQ. Accordingly, once the organization weakened, it looked as though the movement was out of steam. But it was the organization that was out of steam, not the movement.

The Meech Lake episode offered a great opportunity for the PQ to reorganize itself, to promote its cause, and to bolster its support among the electorate.[6] It could mobilize its members and gain additional support among those who sympathized with the sovereignty-association cause. It should be noted that as long as there was consensus on the accord, many pro-independence Quebecers opposed it, as recorded in newspaper accounts.[7] But when opposition to it grew in English-speaking Canada, they changed their position. As a Quebec commentator observed, the reaction was: "If English-speaking Canadians are opposed to it, then it must contain something valuable for us!"[8]

The accord also provided an opportunity for the creation or growth of new political groups: the Reform Party and the Bloc québécois. Other interests got involved, such as women's groups, native peoples, Northerners, ethnic and linguistic minorities, as well as anglophone fringe groups such as the Alliance for the Preservation of English in Canada (APEC),[9] the Confederation of Regions Party (CoR), and the Equality Party, formed in Quebec in response to Bill 178.[10]

---

6 On this, see Lise Bissonnette, *Le Devoir* (Montreal), March 12, 1988.

7 See, for example, articles in *Le Devoir* (Montreal) on June 4 and 6, 1987, January 19 and 20, 1988, and March 12, 1988.

8 Bissonnette, *Le Devoir* (Montreal), March 12, 1988.

9 That particular events and statements by public authorities can create political opportunities is illustrated by the APEC president's reaction to the premier of Alberta's call for the abolition of official bilingualism. He declared that the premier's remarks "put us right back in the ball game again" (*Maclean's*, January 20, 1992.

10 Four Equality Party candidates were elected in the September 1989 election in Quebec.

These groups were among the driving forces in the evolution of the Meech Lake episode: they interpreted it for their respective constituencies, analyzed each other's reactions, and defined what was acceptable and objectionable in the pronouncements of government officials.

Even though the conflicts between English- and French-speaking Canadians and between Quebec and the rest of Canada have occupied a prominent place in public affairs during the past 30 years, other movements were also pressuring for social and institutional change during the same period. A new consciousness and political organization emerged among native peoples and is likely to have a profound and long-lasting impact on the social and political structure of Canadian society. Feminism also acquired momentum, as did the environmental movement and multiculturalism.

A 1990 survey showed that more than three-quarters of the citizens' groups dealing with environmental, multicultural, native and women's issues have been founded since 1960.[11] Until the 1960s, native peoples, women, many ethnic minorities, and Northerners had been relatively marginal to the political process in Canada, if not entirely excluded from it. But the cultural and political awakening that took place throughout the Western world in that decade spawned a large number of groups and organizations that continue to be socially and politically active. The 1982 Charter of Rights and Freedoms then gave them additional legitimation and encouragement.[12] Naturally, these groups too were drawn into the process of constitutional change.

---

11 The survey was conducted by Patrick A. McCartney, "An Examination of Federal and Provincial Government Sponsorship of Voluntary Associations in Canada" (Queen's University, Kingston, Ont., M.A. thesis, 1990, Mimeographed), and quoted in Alan C. Cairns, *Disruptions: Constitutional Struggles from the Charter to Meech Lake* (Toronto: McClelland & Stewart, 1991), p. 20.

12 Alan Cairns (*Disruptions*) uses the expression "Charter Canadians" to refer to these groups. He claims that they define their citizenship on the basis of rights established in the Charter. Not that they did not have the right to participate in the political process before the Charter; rather, the Charter has given them a new political consciousness and is thus a further impetus to political involvement.

There were also expressions of alienation in Western Canada and anxiety in Atlantic Canada over the underdevelopment of that region's economy. These, of course, were not new, but the emphasis placed on the question of "national unity" — that is, to Quebec's grievances and the threat of independence — increased the feeling that problems beyond Central Canada were being ignored. As this was also a period of province-building — as shown by the growth of provincial governments relative to the federal government — provincial politicians encouraged these expressions of alienation. Not surprisingly, provincial concerns and aspirations also found their way into the constitutional debate.

Some groups saw the accord as an opportunity to further gains already made, while others sought to reverse earlier changes. Francophones and several ethnic groups felt that, as a result of past changes, their own culture, language, and collective identity had gained recognition and status. But their aspirations were not wholly satisfied. Indeed, for Quebec francophones, the accord was seen as a means of bringing society and its institutional matrix into greater conformity with their own cultural-symbolic views and aspirations.

Others, including many English-speakers, experienced the past changes as a decline in their sociocultural status and dominance. It was to them that the Reform Party, APEC, and CoR appealed.[13] For them, the Canada that was emerging as a result of these changes was not the one with which they had always identified.

Some in Central Canada felt that they had been displaced by francophones and ethnocultural groups as the central definers of the symbolic-cultural character of Canadian society and as the dominant influence in institutional decisionmaking, and they resented it. In other regions of the country, particularly the West, the feeling was not one of displacement but of being left out of the process entirely. The changes were initiated by Central Canadians who had no intention of paying attention to the concerns of the West. This was yet another instance of the West's general political marginalization.

---

13 The lack of data on the membership and supporters of these parties and organizations makes it difficult to specify the social basis of their support.

The resentment was intensified by continuous reminders of this displacement and marginality. During the debate in 1988 over changes in the *Official Languages Act*, those who questioned the changes were called "dinosaurs," a label that even appeared in headlines, as in "Language Bill Survives Dinosaur Bite."[14] Newspaper reports on the new legislation clearly highlighted this sense of being ignored — for example, "another language fight lost."[15]

Many believed that an official definition of Canada as a nation of two founding peoples would be a symbolic gain for Quebec over and above those it had already made in earlier negotiations. Such a definition would give Quebec a special status in the country. In addition, the situation was seen as a zero-sum game: one side's gains would be the other's losses. The proposed changes were therefore strongly resisted.

Some of those who had lost influence eventually came to see the accord as an occasion to re-enter the public scene, recoup earlier symbolic losses and reestablish power in national decisionmaking. They took it as an opportunity to challenge policies of bilingualism and multiculturalism, the definition of society underlying these policies, and the distribution of power that brought them about.

Especially in the West, the issue of the distribution of power with regard to Quebec was generalized to the entire political system. The content of the accord and the ratification process symbolized the inadequacy of the entire system of representation and policymaking at the national level. One of the main criticisms was that by concentrating enormous power in the cabinet and the office of the prime minister, the system made authoritarian policymaking possible. By their very structure, institutions were failing to represent fairly the different groups and regions of the country. In the West, a reformed Senate was considered a possible solution.

Clearly, a wide range of political actors saw opportunities. Some extreme objectives, strategies, tactics, and rhetoric were adopted, and

14 *The Globe and Mail* (Toronto), June 11, 1988.

15 *Western Report*, July 1988, p. 12.

not only by extremists. There were also touches of extremism in the verbal strategies of some mainstream groups and leaders, including the political authorities themselves. Through the mass media, extremism intensified the controversy by casting the issues in dogmatic terms and raising the emotional pitch of the public debate.

Conclusion

People who institute change must take four sets of political factors into account: (1) gains and losses incidental to policymaking; (2) the timing of policy initiatives; (3) the legitimacy of change; and (4) policymaking as a three-part process.

Gains and Losses Incidental to Policymaking

An important step in policymaking is to identify the interests that are likely to be activated by the proposed policy. This includes taking historical and sociopolitical factors into account. An error in estimating the degree of risk involved jeopardizes the project, especially if there is a long time between the initiation of the process and its final ratification.

The Timing of Policy Initiatives

When the risk of failure is substantial, policymakers try either to avoid the issue entirely or to postpone intervention until a more opportune occasion presents itself. They can delay action, for example, by setting up task forces or Royal Commissions to examine the issue. Such mechanisms take different points of view into account, lower the emotional level, and temper the intensity of ideological fervor.

Policymakers may, of course, have little choice. A crisis or intense political pressure may force them to take immediate action. This, however, was not the situation in the case of Meech Lake. There was no widespread popular pressure to act on the Constitution at the time. Some political authorities felt that the matter had to be dealt with to make it possible for them to go on to deal with other constitutional issues, such as the question of aboriginal self-government. But there was no impending crisis.

Some argued that precisely because there was no imminent crisis, the time was ripe to proceed with a round of negotiations that would include Quebec in the Constitution from both a political — its exclusion was largely self-imposed as a protest — and a social-psychological point of view — Quebec was never excluded legally from the Constitution. Others felt that more time should elapse before the Constitution entered the political agenda. Provincial and federal authorities received warnings of the dangers involved from a number of different sources.[16]

Given the sociopolitical situation, the recent history of controversies and the advice received, the political authorities should have expected the controversy that ensued. Perhaps it was their fear of a controversy that prompted them to adopt a strategy of secrecy both before and during the negotiations and to avoid a public debate afterward.

In view of the residuum of past controversies, all constitution-making should now be suspended for an extended period. Indeed, the Meech Lake controversy has not only resurrected memories of previous confrontations but has added significantly to them. Latent tensions could easily surface again. New proposals may provide an opportunity for groups with a counteragenda that could, once more, set the confrontational process in motion. The risks are still high.

Legality and Legitimacy

The influence of policymakers on the escalation or containment of a conflict is in part determined by the procedures they establish for discussing and adopting a policy. In particular, the way opponents

---

16 See Cohen, *A Deal Undone,* pp. 79–80.

are treated is critical, especially if it is seen as a violation of basic democratic values.

This is the case even if the procedure followed is entirely legal. The law did not oblige the authorities to consult the citizens through public hearings, for example, before arriving at a final proposal. In question was the legitimacy of the process: its validity in relation to generally accepted social values.

Policymaking: A Three-Part Process

Negotiating public policy involves three kinds of bargaining. First, political authorities and their advisers negotiate in federal-provincial meetings, task forces, and other kinds of committees. The negotiators are the representatives of collectivities whose interests they are expected to defend or promote. They must design a plan that is satisfactory both technically, in that it deals effectively with the issues, and politically, in that it is acceptable to the various parties concerned. This is the formal and planned component of sociopolitical bargaining.

Some government leaders and analysts see Confederation as a pact between governments, not between peoples or societies.[17] This may have been a traditionally acceptable view, but the Meech Lake episode clearly showed that it is not socially valid any more. The second kind of bargaining takes place among groups of citizens who are concerned with the issue. Subgroups and their leaders articulate opinions on the positions of other groups and on that of the government, pollsters survey opinions and attitudes, and academics and other social analysts make analyses. This public discussion is a form of bargaining through which each group learns what others want

---

17 This view was explicitly expressed during the 1982 negotiations over the patriation of the Constitution. Some premiers opposed the federal proposal for a referendum on the grounds that the pact was between governments and should therefore be modified only by governments, without the involvement of the population.

from the negotiations, how strongly they feel about the issues and what compromises they are prepared to make.

As there is little direct communication between people in franco-phone Quebec and those in English-speaking Canada, much of this exchange of messages takes place through the media. Internal com-munications may be equally if not more important in shaping inter-group bargaining than messages intended for the other group. Perception is selective: to some extent, people hear or see what fits their mentality and emotional predisposition. But communication that occurs through the media is doubly selective, since those who run the media make an initial selection. They choose to present some events and pronouncements and ignore others, or to emphasize some and play down others.

Third, bargaining takes place between political authorities and their constituencies. For negotiations to be successful, elites must arrive at a settlement that will be accepted by their constituents.[18] Their authority as group representatives must not be seriously challenged, and they must be able to generate a consensus within their own constituencies over the negotiated arrangement. The process of con-vincing the constituents of the value of the formally negotiated package is a form of bargaining. Leaders may carry out a propaganda campaign for this purpose. But there are limits to persuasion by this means, especially in a democracy. Leaders have to take the views, aspirations, or demands of groups in their own constituencies seriously.

Although the first kind of bargaining is the only formal process, the three forms are so intertwined that the outcome can depend at least as much on the informal as on the formal processes.[19] This is the case in terms of both legal ratification and its social *legitimacy*.

---

18 See, for example, Samuel B. Bacharach and Edward J. Lawler, *Power and Politics in Organizations* (San Francisco: Jossey-Bass, 1981); Morton Deutsch, "Conflicts: Productive and Destructive," *Journal of Social Issues* 25 (1969): 7–41; Arend Lijp-hart, "Consociational Democracy," *World Politics* 21 (1969): 207–225; and Eric A. Nordlinger, *Conflict Regulation in Divided Societies* (Cambridge, Mass.: Harvard University, Center for International Affairs, 1972).

19 On the distinction between formal and informal processes, see, for example, Bacharach and Lawler *Power and Politics in Organizations*; and Thomas Schelling, *The Strategy of Conflict* (Cambridge, Mass.: Harvard University Press, 1975)....

Formal and informal processes may not be concurrent. The informal processes may be well under way by the time the formal negotiations begin and continue while the latter are going on. The reverse can also occur, as the evolution of the Meech Lake episode shows: the informal bargaining among different segments of the population and between them and their governments began after the formal process was complete. The political authorities had not anticipated this or else they believed it was manageable.

What happens in the formal negotiations — or what appears to be happening, since formal negotiations are usually carried out in secret — what is said, and not said, by the representatives of each constituency to justify the agreement, and the way these representatives treat those who oppose the deal may all influence the informal bargaining. This is the case whether political authorities behave spontaneously or as part of a strategy to manage consensus.

If the issues at stake are important enough to them, members of affected constituencies will to react to the formal process and the way it is carried out. They will react to the verbal and nonverbal behavior of authorities and to the gains and losses they are likely to incur relative to other constituencies as a result of the new arrangement.

Similarly, what is expressed through the informal bargaining — attitudes, opinions, emotions, imputation of motives, arguments justifying or opposing the agreement — can be crucial for the evolution and outcome of the bargaining. Informal transactions may open possibilities of exchange and facilitate compromise, or else lead to extreme demands, intransigence, and hostility, rendering compromise impossible.

Informal processes acquire crucial importance when intergroup confrontations have occurred in the recent past. Such a history

---

Note 19 - cont'd.

...Negotiations among political authorities, although they are carried out within a formal framework, also have an informal component. Indeed, the personalities of the individuals involved, their ideological orientations, their understanding of the issues, their political affiliations, the likes and dislikes they have for one other as individuals, and the sociopsychological dynamics of their interaction can all affect the evolution and outcome of the formal negotiations. This, as Cohen (*A Deal Undone*) shows, was clearly the case in the Meech Lake negotiations.

sets limits on what authorities can convincingly propose to their own constituents and on what members of other collectivities are likely to accept.

In short, whether or not the authorities have planned for public participation, the public is likely to participate in the constitution-making process, especially when the issues at stake go beyond economic and political interests and involve definitions of collective identity. This was clearly the case with the Meech Lake episode.

Chapter 3

Change and Intergroup Conflict

A combination of symbolic and political processes ignited the controversy over the Meech Lake Accord. But once under way, a controversy has a dynamic of its own.[1]

The evolution of social controversy is characterized by progressive social and attitudinal polarization. These are complex phenomena. Social divisions deepen, and individuals take increasingly emotional and one-sided positions. They cease to consider the complexity of the issues, and increasingly respond to events by stereotyping, oversimplifying the other's position, and applying selective memory to what was said and done.

Factors underlying Social Polarization

This section discusses four factors underlying polarization:[2]

- increased communication blocks among the various groups involved;
- the use of loaded language;
- the shift from issues to attacks on individuals and groups; and
- the growing influence of militants and extremists.[3]

---

1 See James S. Coleman, *Community Conflict* (Glencoe, Ill.: Free Press, 1957).

2 Other conditions, such as the occurrence of climate-creating events, discussed in Chapter 1, can also contribute to social and psychological polarization.

3 On social and attitudinal polarization, see Coleman, *Community Conflict*; William A. Gamson, "Rancorous Conflict in Community Politics," *American Sociological Review* 31 (1966): 71–80; and Anthony Oberschall, *Social Conflict and Social Movements* (Englewood Cliffs, N.J.: Prentice-Hall, 1973).

Communication Blocks

One explanation for the growing conflict during the Meech Lake episode was a lack of communication among the principal groups involved. In fact, there was plenty of communication, but the competitive struggle for political and symbolic advantage determined *what* was communicated. On the one hand, people focused on factors that justified their position, on how fair and reasonable it was, and on the noble motives underlying it. On the other hand, they drew attention to the weakness of the other side's position by showing that it was inequitable, unreasonable, and based on selfishness, prejudice, and hostility. Each side communicated the negative aspects of the other's character and attitudes.

Members of each collectivity ignored the positive aspects of their common history: the accommodations worked out in the past and the accumulated stock of goodwill. If attention was drawn to these, they were dismissed as irrelevant ("too little, too late") or as examples of the unreasonableness of the opponent ("this goes on and on; they are never satisfied"). As many observers have noted, there is a profound gap between the two collectivities because of their ignorance of each other. But there is more than ignorance: the recurrent tensions between them tend to focus each other's attention on the negative rather than on the positive.

The Use of Loaded Language

Much of the Meech Lake debate centered on the issues. But there was a fair dose of contamination in verbal exchanges among the participants, especially over the "distinct society" clause.

Arguments such as the one that Quebec had been a distinct society for more than 200 years raised more questions than it answered: if that was the case (as almost no one would deny), why the desire to constitutionalize this reality now? The argument had the unintended result of confirming the suspicion that "distinct society" was a code word for "special status" and not simply recognition of a social and cultural reality.

Defenders of the accord used language that was symbolically and emotionally loaded. Quebec refused to be treated as a minority, and it was to be able to sign the Constitution with honor; it would not accept *un fédéralisme à genoux*, a federalism on its knees — an expression frequently used by Quebec politicians. Such verbal strategies shifted the debate to a different plane. Instead of focusing attention on the merits of the proposed measures and on the problems they were meant to address, they defined the debate as one of recognition and respect. Failure to ratify the accord would thus be a rejection and a humiliation, not a simple disagreement over a policy.

Verbal strategies included threats — of separation, of economic retaliation — sometimes in emotionally provocative language. Thus, Quebec political scientist Léon Dion said that English Canada would negotiate only with "a knife at its throat." Threats called for counterthreats, and the confrontation escalated. In English-speaking Canada, explicit threats were made about to the geographic boundaries of Quebec were it to become independent. It was indicated that there would be no economic association or, at the least, negotiations would be difficult. It was also pointed out that there would be retaliation, as people would react very strongly to the breakup of their country.

There is a rationale to threats: they draw attention to the possible costs of the other party's position. As such they may induce compromise. But in the climate of the Meech Lake controversy, at the height of ideological and emotional fervor, they had the opposite effect. They led not to modifications but to a hardening of positions, not to rapprochement but to polarization.

Each side perceives its own arguments as realistic assessments of the situation and its opponents' arguments as threats — although the phrase "a knife at its throat" was unmistakable for both sides. For instance, in 1991 a Quebec analyst, oblivious to the fact that threats of independence have been a constant feature of political discourse in Quebec for quite some time, criticized an aboriginal leader for using threats "in a province that is oversensitive to symbolism."[4]

---

4 *The Globe and Mail* (Toronto), October 24, 1991.

Considering the symbolically and emotionally loaded character of the public discourse, many of the private conversations and
debates that took place in the living rooms, bars, and on the front
porches of the country were no doubt even more intense in content
and tone. Privately, the epithets used to characterize the opponent
would be harsher, the stereotyping and prejudice less restrained, the
threats more extreme, the other side's strategies seen as more cynical,
and their motives regarded as more ignoble. The polarization
reached deep into people's psyches.

From Issues to Individuals and Groups

Ad hominem arguments usually emerge in political debates. The
Meech Lake debate was no exception, but in this instance the ratio
of *ad hominem* to issue-related arguments increased until it became a
central feature of the debate. Once people started labeling and
accusing one another, the process escalated on its own, with each
assertion triggering a response, and deteriorated into a spiral of
hostility.

The purpose of using *ad hominem* arguments is to delegitimate
opponents. The opponent is shown to be arrogant, unreasonable,
self-interested, unfair, biased, or hiding some questionable objective.
If such accusations are valid, the reasoning runs, then the legitimacy
of the opponent's stand also becomes dubious and can be discarded.

During the Meech Lake controversy, suspicions about motives
were expressed, the attitudes of the other side were attacked, its
morality was challenged, and undesirable personality traits were
identified. These attacks were made on the motives and character
not only of first ministers supporting or opposing the accord and of
other proponents and opponents but also of entire groups such as
Quebec, English Canada, and the "dissident provinces."

Suspicions of Government Intentions

From the outset, people in English Canada were suspicious of the
intentions of the governments in Ottawa and Quebec City. They were

seen as being in collusion, as having engineered the whole project with a particular purpose in mind, as conspiring to make a special deal for Quebec. The prime minister was already partisan, and the accord was another bow to Quebec. The presence of Quebec nationalists and *indépendantistes* made his party and government appear even more suspect. Some thought that, through his "wheeling and dealing," he was giving more to Quebec than most Quebecers even wanted.

On the other hand, some pro-independence Quebecers accused the federal government of attempting, with the support of the anglophone majority, to put Quebec in its place. They accused their own government of being an accomplice in this shrewd English-Canadian maneuver.

An early criticism was that the premiers went to Meech to get something for themselves rather than to deal with a national problem. While they were proclaiming the importance of bringing Quebec fully into the Canadian family, they were really concerned with the additional powers they could acquire. Some suspected that the concern with a reformed Senate was activated by Western premiers because they could not satisfactorily explain their support for the accord and needed a platform to deal with public dissatisfaction.

Most people would probably agree that the first responsibility of premiers is to their provinces. Yet critics complained that none of the premiers was concerned primarily about the country as a whole. Critics even observed that the federal authorities seemed prepared to decentralize even if it meant the dismemberment of the country. Some linked the accord with the Canada-U.S. Free Trade Agreement: in different ways, both were eroding the fabric of the country.

The perception was widespread that the whole exercise was one of cynical political tinkering and manipulation, a suspicion that was confirmed for many by the prime minister's description of the climactic first ministers' meeting in June 1990 as a "roll of the dice" — an expression that has become a symbol of this way of proceeding.

In segmented societies, the elites of the various segments must be committed to making the institutional system work and to reinforcing society's cohesion. If important subgroups in the elite are seen as unwilling (not just unable) to make this commitment, the level of suspicion and cynicism increases. In spite of the rhetoric, the main participants in the negotiations were criticized as caring more about pursuing limited or partisan interests than the interest of the country as a whole.

The accuracy of these perceptions and criticisms is not the concern here. As the controversy went on, the perceptions may well have been distorted and the criticisms vastly exaggerated, but they became generally accepted as correct. This is what happens in a controversy. They reflected a real problem of public confidence in the willingness of political leaders to assume responsibility for the country as a whole and not just for group interests, the electoral fate of their parties and the pursuit of political power.

Accusations against Opponents

Some opponents of the accord were accused of harboring hidden motives. Women's groups, for example, were accused of using equality rights as an excuse to oppose the recognition of Quebec as a distinct society: "A lot of people are using that as a Trojan horse, not because they're trying to protect women's rights, but because they don't want a distinct society and the Meech Lake Accord."[5] Much of the resistance to the accord was perceived as anti-Quebec, as a refusal to recognize its distinctiveness, as racist — an emotionally loaded term if there is one nowadays — and as malicious and hostile.

Generalizations to the Entire Collectivity

Accusations about the personality traits of political leaders quickly extended to the entire collectivity. Thus, Quebec was described as

---

5 *The Globe and Mail* (Toronto), August 20, 1987. The statement is by the prime minister, although he attributes it to a columnist of the Montreal newspaper *La Presse*.

arrogant and inflexible, as self-centered, tribal, and interested in Canada only if it pays. Like a "disturbed youngster,"[6] it was never satisfied.

Quebecers tended to attribute these expressions of prejudice and hostility to all English Canadians, who were then accused of being indifferent to Quebec's cultural predicament. They were denounced as smug and prejudiced. They were said to want to "put Quebec in its place." English Canada was described as internally divided, with no coherent cultural identity, but at the same time as united in its hostility to Quebec and French.[7]

Perceived Lack of Reciprocity

A perceived lack of reciprocal accommodation was one of the fundamental issues of the controversy, and it relates to the basic character of the relationship between French-speaking Quebecers and English-speaking Canadians. Lack of reciprocity was perceived and resented on both sides. Quebecers felt that while they had voted for Canada by rejecting sovereignty-association in the 1980 referendum, English-speaking Canadians were not reciprocating by accepting the Meech Lake Accord.

Resentment was equally intense among those English-speaking Canadians who earlier had supported reforms to rectify Quebec's grievances — and those of francophones in general — and had adopted the project of a bilingual Canada. For them, the main problem was Quebec's lack of interest in Canada. They saw Quebec as interested in Canada only for what it could get out of it, with no sense of obligation toward any other part of the country. Some premiers indicated that negotiations were impossible until Quebec demonstrated its commitment to the country. Quebec politicians "should say something more inspiring about Canada than simply

---

6 Don McGillivray, *Ottawa Citizen*, September 25, 1989.

7 For an interesting description and analysis of these images of English Canada, see Jeffrey Simpson, *The Globe and Mail* (Toronto), December 22, 1990.

that they'll keep it as long as it lays golden eggs."[8] The language of *fédéralisme rentable* or "profitable federalism" on the part of Quebec politicians and the calculating attitude it implied was offensive. It expressed a balance-sheet, profit-and-loss attitude toward the country.

Quebecers were felt to be largely unaware of the degree to which English Canada had already accepted French and Quebec's cultural distinctiveness, of the extent to which anglophones were ready to make institutional accommodations, and of the changes that had taken place over the past 30 years. The view of some Quebecers that it was only with Meech Lake that English-speaking Canadians were waking up to Quebec and to the need for changes in federal institutions was received with complete disbelief. As one author wrote, "Not enough serious talk about Quebec's place in Canada? Good grief — have the rest of us been hallucinating for the past three decades?"[9]

Double Standards

The issue of double standards was raised more often by francophone Quebecers than by English-speaking Canadians, especially in connection with Bill 178 on the language of commercial signs. Francophones saw the negative response of many English-speaking Canadians as based on standards different from those they apply to the language policies of English-speaking provinces. Francophone Quebecers felt that English-speaking provinces were demanding rights for Quebec anglophones that they were not prepared to grant to their own minorities. This was experienced as particularly offensive when coming from provinces that had strongly resisted the introduction of measures supporting the French language and culture.

The perceptions of Quebec francophones in this regard were not entirely inaccurate. A recent survey has shown that 97 percent of

---

8 Charles Lynch, *Ottawa Citizen*, October 1, 1989.

9 George Galt, "Can't Live with Them; Can't Live without Them," *Saturday Night*, June 1991.

anglophones "support the right of anglophones living in Quebec, but only 65 percent support the same right of francophones living outside Quebec."[10] (Among francophones, the corresponding figures are 91 percent and 96 percent.)

Another perception of a double standard by Quebecers was that it was seen as acceptable for English-speaking provinces to pursue what they perceived as in their best interests, but when Quebec sought to do the same it was defined as the pursuit of privileges. Meanwhile, English Canadians criticized the fact that so much pressure was applied on English Canada to accept the accord but little on Quebec to accept the modifications needed to meet the concerns expressed.

The Growing Influence of Militants and Extremists

In a controversy, militants and extremists acquire an importance that is disproportionate to their number in the population. This is partly due, as discussed earlier, to wavering public confidence in political authorities and to the fact that public authorities themselves use emotionally loaded language, thereby legitimating its use by others.

The media also boost the influence of militants and extremists. Extremist behavior serves the media's interest in gaining and maintaining an audience and may also serve the political interests of those who control or run the media. The regular reporting of extreme statements and behavior contributes to the process of polarization, both social and psychological. By giving prominence to combative statements and fanatical acts, the media can cause extreme views to be taken as the views of most or all of the collectivity. This feeds the spiral of hostility.

---

10 Paul M. Sniderman et al., "Political Culture and the Problem of Double Standards: Mass and Elite Attitudes toward Language Rights in the Canadian Charter of Rights and Freedoms," *Canadian Journal of Political Science* 22 (1989): 259–284.

Perhaps the most striking manifestation of this phenomenon was the now-infamous Quebec flag incident in Brockville, Ontario. To desecrate a group symbol is to degrade and humiliate that group. The media gave the event enormous significance by showing it repeatedly on television, triggering fury in Quebec and adding momentum to the polarization of attitudes in the country.

Leaders of extreme groups also gain influence because they provide a language for the public expression of complaints, criticisms, and accusations. The other side then responds even more bitingly. The process feeds on itself, generating increasingly distorted perceptions of the other side's goals and strategies. Extreme views and feelings acquire a certain respectability, since they become part of the weaponry of what is perceived as justified political combat. The norms of restraint as to what can be voiced publicly are partly suspended.

Outcomes of Polarization

People come to divide the world into "us" and "them," the heroes and the villains. Negative perceptions become increasingly generalized. People give less and less acknowledgment to diversity of opinion in the population and among the political elites. It is only those who were "against us" that count, not those who are prepared to compromise or even support "our" position. There is also a sociopolitical dynamic. Insofar as leaders on each side convince the opposition that their constituents are all behind them, they too contribute to the process of polarization.

Sociopolitical polarization falls under Gresham's Law of Conflict, according to which extremists drive out those who are prepared to compromise and moderates progressively disappear from the political scene. As James Coleman described the process, "The forces put into effect by the initiation of the conflict act to drive out the conciliatory elements, [and] replace them with those better equipped for combat." Less restrained leaders attempt to mobilize support. More aggressive organizations "arise to replace the milder, more constrained pre-existing organizations; derogatory and scurrilous charges replace dispassionate issues; antagonism replaces disagreement, and a drive to ruin the opponent takes the place of the initial will to win."[11]

The Meech Lake episode fits Coleman's description. People became obsessed with what had gone wrong and ignored what had been working satisfactorily. The accumulated goodwill of the past was ignored. Efforts that had made to accommodate the other groups and the benefits of those efforts were deemed irrelevant. The advantages of a culturally diverse society were minimized or negated. The advantages of a federal regime were played down and its constraints magnified.

Conclusion

The analysis presented here prompts the following considerations.

Loaded Language

What political authorities say can be of strategic importance simply because they are in positions of authority. The kind of language they use can affect the evolution of events. Political authorities must therefore consider the possible effect of what they say, what underlying messages they may be communicating to the public.

Verbal and nonverbal behavior can have a long-term as well as a short-term effect. In the long term, it may create either a favorable or an adverse climate for public debate and the accommodation of different points of view. Short-term and long-term effects are sometimes at odds with each other. An argument that seems appropriate and even persuasive in the short term could have negative long-term effects by evoking latent antagonisms that change the climate of the debate. "A strategy of verbal behavior that fails to keep the longer

---

11 Coleman, *Community Conflict*, p. 14.

range of impact in focus can be costly, no matter how successful it is in helping in any single encounter."[12]

The behavior of both political and social authorities can be crucial. Among social opinionmakers, the media are particularly prone to sacrifice long-term effect for short-term gain.

Verbal behavior is particularly influential in nascent confrontations. "Crisis management signals" given by authorities can, over time, "succeed in transforming a whole pattern of interaction, instance by instance, or in reinforcing an existing pattern of conduct," or they can result in "unintended and unwelcome fallout."[13]

Threats and statements that arouse guilt feelings are examples of this kind of verbal behavior. They may appear convincing — they might even force people on the other side to change their minds — but they change the tone of a debate. Most people know from their own experience the effect of a threat or an accusation on the nature of a discussion in a small group: it can transform a discussion into a shouting match. The process is the same at the level of political debate.

Verbal behavior can also have a long-term influence on the expression of extremist views. Public authorities who use emotionally loaded language to convince opponents of the value of their proposal may find it has the opposite effect, because it provokes the use of similar language on their part.

Ambiguity

Ambiguity is a double-edged sword. It can be a powerful tool in the hands of those in power, but it can also undermine the very project undertaken. It is risky because it is open to various interpretations. Ambiguity can make people suspicious: What hidden motives does it conceal?

Its sociopolitical effect can be particularly detrimental if it is perceived as concealing a paradigmatic change in the character of

---

12 Thomas M. Franck and Edward Weisband, *Verbal Strategies among the Superpowers* (New York: Oxford University Press, 1971), p. 122.

13 Ibid., p. 125.

the society. Basic definitions of the social order should not necessarily be avoided; on the contrary, they may be necessary. The way in which such changes are managed is critical, however, and ambiguity that generates suspicions can prevent rather than facilitate the change. Adequately informing citizens, it should be noted, is a basic requirement of democracy — even though politicians frequently ignore it on the grounds that "citizens would not understand."

Diversity and Status

When political authorities intervene to allocate recognition or status among groups,[14] the groups will start to compare gains and losses. The singling out of a collectivity or province in a policy almost inevitably leads others to examine what it could imply for them in terms of status, power, or economic benefits.[15] The level of competition and envy increases among the groups, and the ensuing tensions can damage society's cohesion and its political stability. Recognition and status are not easily negotiable, in contrast to means-ends policies.

The Meech Lake experience suggests that the Constitution is not an appropriate vehicle for the recognition of groups in a highly differentiated society. Trying to do so creates more problems than it solves. There are other ways in which the cultural or other specificities of groups can be acknowledged in a society, without provoking destructive, envy-creating comparisons among the groups. This implication of the Meech Lake episode is discussed further in the next chapter.

14 On this aspect of the Meech Lake episode, see Evelyn Kallen, "The Meech Lake Accord: Entrenching a Pecking Order of Minority Rights," *Canadian Public Policy* 14 (1988): S107–S120.

15 Raymond Breton, "Multiculturalism and Canadian Nation-Building," in Alan Cairns and Cynthia Williams, eds., *The Politics of Gender, Ethnicity and Language in Canada* (Toronto: University of Toronto Press, 1986), pp. 27–66.

Chapter 4

The Failure to Reconcile the Irreconcilable

Why did the political authorities fail to convince Canadians that the Meech Lake Accord was needed? Perhaps this was simply an impossible task: it meant reconciling the irreconcilable.

No complex, highly differentiated society is free of contradictions and divergences in its social, economic, and political organization. They are the result of historical antecedents, variations in a country's geography and climate, and demographic conditions. No society is without its cultural contradictions either. These may manifest themselves when the practical implications of the worldviews and aspirations of different segments of the population are spelled out. Even generally shared values may have contradictory practical implications — for example, the values of economic growth and redistribution of wealth. The idea that a society can eliminate its structural and cultural contradictions and related social tensions is a fantasy. Rapid social change also makes unrealistic the idea that contradictions can be dealt with once and for all.

Contradictions in Canadian Society

Canadian society is no exception to the general rule: it contains many contradictions that, under some conditions, are translated into sociopolitical tension. Some of these surfaced during the Meech Lake episode because the architects of the accord introduced them, perhaps not intentionally, into the public debate. Others surfaced because groups exploited these contradictions for their political advantage. A few of these contradictions will be discussed briefly in the following pages.

Nations, Regions, and Provinces

Canadians have been unable so far to find a final, once-and-for-all accommodation of these different principles. Yet judging from the terms used in Canadian political discourse, Canada includes them all. In addition to the two-founding-nations expression, Canada is described as a bilingual society. We talk of language communities, English and French Canada, Quebec and the rest of Canada. We speak of First Nations, and of regions as well as provinces. We refer to the specific geographic parts of the country, such as the West, the Prairies, the Maritimes, and Atlantic Canada.

Few people would deny the existence of these different realities. The debate concerns how they are to be incorporated into the organization of political institutions, because it is at this level that contradictions may be felt. Thus, attempts to incorporate one of these realities is frequently seen as detrimental to another and therefore as a threat to its existence and vitality.

This tension has appeared in the debate over the notion of Quebec as a distinct society on the one hand and the equality of the provinces on the other — a tension that cannot be resolved by simply rejecting one of these two dimensions of reality. Some seem to favor such a solution: supporters of independence in Quebec, the Reform Party — which has adopted a variation of the two-founding-nations idea — and those English Canadians who argue that English Canada would be better off without Quebec.

The "distinct society" clause of the Meech Lake Accord was usually thought of as referring to Quebec. It did. But it also referred to Canada — Quebec was defined as distinct *within* Canada. The significance of this statement for the character of Canada as a society was not spelled out. There was much debate about its legal but not its sociological implications, even though it was essentially a statement about the character of Canadian society and about how its different segments fit together. Many people were uncomfortable with that statement, and others rejected it completely.

As the controversy evolved, the very character of Canadian society emerged as the underlying issue. It became apparent for many that the accord and the recognition of Quebec as a distinct society was a disguised affirmation of what francophone Quebecers consider to be the only historically and socially valid view of Canada and of their place in it: the view of Canada as a society of two nations, with francophones as one of the founding peoples. This is partly why the distinct society notion is so highly valued in Quebec.

But that is also why it was viewed with misgivings in English-speaking Canada. The distinct society concept as a reformulation or repackaging of the two-founding-nations theory was seen as giving a special status to Quebec relative to other parts of the country. The symbolic representation of Canadian society and the structuring of its institutions according to a paradigm based on two nations and two founding peoples is at odds with the principle of the equality of the provinces. This contradiction is felt particularly strongly in the West, which has gained demographic and economic importance in recent decades and accordingly aspires to appropriate social and political recognition. Such a representation is also at odds with the historical reality of the participation of the native peoples in the founding of Canada.

From the occasional reference by Quebec politicians to a political superstructure overarching Quebec and the rest of Canada, many sensed that the accord was not simply a proposal about specific changes in certain policy areas. Rather, the underlying intention was to redefine the character of the society, entailing a radical transformation of the country's institutional structure on the basis of the two-founding-nations idea. Thus, the accord brought to the surface an issue that has emerged regularly in one form or another throughout the history of Canada. It is an issue that has divided francophone Quebecers among themselves as well as Quebecers and other Canadians. Is Quebec a nation, a province, or both?

Regional Differences

The different parts of Canada have different histories, demogra-
phies, ecologies, economic structures, and political cultures. Their
relationships with each another and with the political and administrative center in Ottawa cannot therefore be the same. Nor do they
experience the same advantages and disadvantages in being part of
a federation — the mixture of opportunities and constraints is different for each region.

Two Western Canadian economists, E.J. Chambers and M.B.
Percy, have identified four types of possible gain from economic
union:

- gain that "derives from the incentives for greater specialization
  of labor and the exploitation of scale economies";
- "the ability to pool risks at the national level to ameliorate the
  consequences of regional instability";
- "the sharing of overhead expenditures on defense,...large-scale
  transportation projects, and similar areas of mutual benefit";
  and
- "the greater market power that an economic union can exert in
  international trade relations."[1]

Chambers and Percy stress that the package of possible benefits is
not the same for each region of the country. In addition, what may
be a set of gains during one period may not be as advantageous in
another.

Some argue that the present arrangements between the Atlantic
provinces and the federal government — for example, the transfer
payments system — are critical components of a social contract

---

1 E.J. Chambers and M.B. Percy, "Natural Resources and the Western Canadian
   Economy: Implications for Constitutional Change," in Norman Cameron et al.,
   From East and West: Regional Views on Reconfederation, The Canada Round 6
   (Toronto: C.D. Howe Institute, 1991), pp. 61–62.

between these provinces and the rest of the country.[2] A similar argument has been made for the less-affluent parts of the West (Manitoba and Saskatchewan), where a "social contract" or "entitlement" view of Canada has emerged over the years.[3] The political culture sees the relationship as involving a *quid pro quo*: in the case of the Atlantic provinces, this means giving up "the right to impose restrictions on the mobility of goods and factors, in return for federal policies designed to encourage economic development in the region and a livelihood for its citizens."[4] There is a concern with sustaining an economy that will prevent massive out-migration from the region and consequent social and political marginalization. In the West, the *quid pro quo* is based on the notion that some federal policies — for example, the National Policy of the nineteenth century — have benefited Central Canada at the expense of the West.[5]

McGill University economist John McCallum speaks of being struck "by the sharp differences in regional perspectives and by the difficulties the federal government is likely to face in trying to reconcile these differences." For example, in contrast to the "social contract" or "entitlement" view of Canada, there is the view that favors a market system based primarily on insurance and stabilization rather than on preserving the present distribution of Canada's population. This difference "may well be the fundamental conflict between Atlantic Canadians and Western Canadians with respect to the Constitution."[6]

---

2 See, for example, Doug May and Dane Rowlands, "Atlantic Canada in Confederation: Uncharted Waters with Dangerous Shoals," in Cameron et al., *From East and West*, pp. 1–56.

3 John McCallum, "Regional Perspectives: Summary and Synthesis," in Cameron et al., *From East and West*, p. 114.

4 May and Rowlands, "Atlantic Canada in Confederation," p. 2.

5 See Norman Cameron, Derek Hum, and Wayne Simpson, "The View from the Less-Affluent West," in Cameron et al., *From East and West*, p. 98.

6 McCallum, "Regional Perspectives," p. 114.

Aboriginality, Ethnocultural Pluralism, and Linguistic Dualism

Aboriginality, ethnocultural pluralism, and linguistic dualism — three fundamental dimensions of Canada's history, demography, and politics — constitute another source of contradictions. In principle, they do not necessarily contradict one other. But in practice, the political aspirations of native peoples for self-government pose difficult problems of accommodation within existing political institutions. The concept of two founding nations denies the native contribution, and many feel it is not compatible with the increasingly multicultural composition of Canadian society and the corresponding decline in the proportion of Canadians of British and French backgrounds.

Similarly, these three dimensions of Canada are seen as contradictory when it comes to particular policy objectives and programs that appear to give special advantages to francophones relative to ethnocultural minorities or to native peoples relative to other Canadians. This is felt particularly strongly in parts of the country where francophones constitute a smaller group than some other ethnocultural minorities, or where native peoples are fairly numerous.

One source of tension is the idea that having come to Canada earlier justifies a special status or that a group's contribution to Canadian society is more valuable and meritorious if it was made earlier rather than later. Some members of ethnic minorities reject special status for any group: we are *all* immigrants in Canada, including the native peoples. The period of migration is rejected as a basis for sociopolitical differentiation. The nature of the contribution to society may be different, but this is a question of circumstances, not merit, and therefore cannot be a legitimate basis for differential status.

On the other hand, the idea that the historical situation of native people — including agreements sealed with binding treaties — justifies special status appears to enjoy a fair degree of support. It is only the nature of that special status and the specific institutional arrangements it requires that are controversial. While the federal government's current constitutional proposals propose that "the right of aboriginal peoples to self-government should be constitutionally recognized," the kinds of difficulties indicated here are explicitly acknowledged, and conditions and procedures are indicated for the specification and implementation of that right.[7] The proposals state that

> it is important to express the nature of the right in terms that guide the courts towards an interpretation of self-government that is consistent with the understanding of both aboriginal and non-aboriginal peoples. Such a right would provide for recognition of the different circumstances and needs of the different aboriginal peoples in Canada.[8]

Thus, when it comes to the institutional implementation of the right to self-government, there are likely to be serious debates over the forms these should take and over the question of "justiciable" versus "inherent" rights. Tensions are likely to occur between native peoples and governments; between federal and provincial governments; between aboriginal and nonaboriginal people; and among aboriginal people themselves. Aboriginal self-government, like the notion of distinct society, does not mean the same thing for everyone. In addition, the application of the right may, in some circumstances, require compromises that are likely to be perceived and experienced by many in the aboriginal collectivity as contradictory to the principle itself.

Individual and Collective Rights

The requirements of collective life and social organization are in constant tension with those of individual autonomy and freedom of

---

7 It is interesting to note that while fairly elaborate conditions and procedures are specified in the case of the right to self-government of native peoples, few are mentioned for the specification of the institutional implications of the recognition of Quebec as a distinct society.

8 Canada, *Shaping Canada's Future Together* (Ottawa: Supply and Services Canada, 1991), p. 7.

choice. The provision and protection of public goods, including language and culture, may constrain the behavior of individual members of the collectivity or impose costs on them.

What can a collectivity legitimately impose on individuals to assure the provision of collective goods? It is political elites that usually decide what public goods are to be pursued and by what means, while charters of individual rights and freedoms set limits on what those elites can do in the pursuit of collective goods.

The legitimate authority of democratically elected leaders should not blind us to the fact that, once in power, governing elites possess considerable power to shape public opinion. There are many situations where members of the political opposition are silenced — for example, by pressures to be "politically correct" — or where they are so much in agreement with their colleagues in power that real opposition ceases to exist. Society's ability to apply critical pressure can also be reduced by rising nationalism, particularly when it is initiated or animated by the political elites themselves. This is often the case when the issue of collective rights is placed on the public agenda.

But are a society's individual rights absolute? Can parents be forced to send their children to school, for instance, or do they have an absolute right to choose? This question gathers intensity when it concerns the rights of the majority and those of minorities. What can a majority legitimately expect from members of minority groups? What claims can a minority make on the majority and on society's institutions?

The tension between individual and collective rights involves several other issues. For instance, who is included in the collectivity, and who is excluded from it? In other words, who is to benefit from the collective rights? If the rights are to be formally recognized, concrete criteria for inclusion and exclusion need to be specified. At this point, serious contradictions with individual rights may arise.

It is not enough to affirm that a particular group has rights. One has to specify what these rights are. Equally important is the question of what costs and constraints the implementation of these rights will entail. A collective right is, by definition, also a set of obligations on someone. Who are those on whom the costs and constraints are to be imposed? To individuals within the collectivity or to those in other collectivities? And in what ways is the collectivity that has rights obligated toward the larger society that recognizes those rights?[9]

The intention here is not to resolve these issues but to point out the need for a philosophy of collective rights, if they are to be part of our political life. Such a philosophy should clarify the limits that individual rights place on the pursuit of collective rights. The intention is also to underscore the fact that most of these issues cannot be resolved once and for all. The tension between the requirements of social, economic, and political organization and those of the autonomy, freedom of choice, and well-being of individuals is present in all societies and must be regularly dealt with as circumstances change and social values evolve.

The federal government's constitutional proposals presented in *Shaping Canada's Future Together* hint at the tension between individual and collective rights:

> Strong arguments have been made that [the notwithstanding clause] dilutes the guarantee of rights under the Charter, since it allows legislatures to exempt themselves from the scope of many (but not all) rights when they deem it necessary. The contrary argument...is that under our parliamentary system it is entirely appropriate that elected representatives, rather than judges, should have the final say *on public policy and social needs*....If it did not exist, judges appointed to the Supreme Court of Canada would be able to determine *the scope of all rights, and any limits to public policy*" [emphasis added].[10]

Centralization and Decentralization

The tension between centralization and decentralization — that is, the question of the distribution of powers among different levels of government — is ever present. Tensions are particularly strong in

---

9 This is not the only other issue involved, only the last one mentioned here.

10 Canada, *Shaping Canada's Future Together*, p. 4.

federal regimes, but they also exist in modern unitary systems that usually contain at least two levels of government — central and municipal or local.

A Canadian variety of this tension is that between sovereignty and association, as each has its own costs and benefits. Economic association may be highly desirable, but it is impossible without delegating or sharing political powers and without being part of a larger political entity. Others may want political sovereignty, but it is not very meaningful when a society is economically weak and dependent.

In other words, societies are wholes. Their different components cannot be separated as if they could function independently of one another. But the two poles of the same reality are likely to be in permanent tension. Debate over the relative merits of sovereignty and association is likely to be a recurrent theme in the politics of modern societies.

A related source of tension in a federal system is the contradiction between formal political equality and actual inequalities of power based on factors such as population size, economic strength, scientific and technological development, and political organization. Again, this contradiction cannot be eliminated except by taking the country apart. As long as these different groups are part of the same federation, the principle of equality will be in contradiction with the actual state of affairs.

Economic Growth and Redistribution of Wealth

Finally, there is the tension between the demands of economic profitability and growth, on the one hand, and social rights on the other.[11] The two are not necessarily incompatible, and both are highly valued in our society, although not equally in all social classes. But since each involves a different allocation of society's resources, which will not

---

11 On the tensions in the application of these values, see Bryan S. Turner, "Outline of a Theory of Citizenship," *Sociology* 24 (1990): 189–217.

benefit all segments of the population equally, the two are often seen as contradictory. It is true that to pursue one value, the other has to be sacrificed to some degree. Difficult choices and compromises are then required.

This source of tension is connected to another pair of related values: individualism and solidarity. Valuing individual autonomy and self-realization may require policies that contradict the value of sharing, mutual support, and obligation to the collectivity. Similarly, policies that emphasize the autonomy, goals, or culture of individual groups and regions may contradict policies that emphasize sharing and support *across* groups and regions in the country.

The "Canada" clause of the federal constitutional proposals set out in *Shaping Canada's Future Together* recognizes these tensions as a "balance that is especially Canadian between personal and collective freedom on the one hand and, on the other hand, the personal and collective responsibility that we all share with each other."[12]

Dealing with
the Contradictions

The idea that, somehow, contradictions can and must be eliminated for society to be better integrated is a myth, even though it is part of the rhetoric used by politicians and militants.

This does not mean that attempts are not made to eliminate or resolve contradictions. For example, potential contradictions may be banished from the public to the private sector (the "privatization bias") or avoided by simply retreating from them (the "retreatist inclination"). Policies and programs may take only one set of values into account, to the detriment of others (the "cultural dominance tendency").

But these attempts tend to accentuate the contradictions, not eliminate them. Contradictions are not arbitrary or the result of some evil force set loose to create trouble. They are embedded in the

---

12 Canada, *Shaping Canada's Future Together*, p. 13.

geography, demography, and socioeconomic structure of society and its larger context. They are also embedded in society's values, and these values have contradictory practical requirements so that pursuing one means sacrificing something of the other.

The Political Activation of Social Contradictions

Social contradictions do not have to be part of the political agenda. They can be accommodated so that they remain latent for a long time. But as they are always present, they will resurface when circumstances change, as the values and goals of various groups evolve, and as institutional changes are made. The tension between the requirements of economic growth and redistribution of wealth, for example, surfaces in periods of economic recession, while in periods of prosperity it is less intense. The tension between linguistic dualism and ethnocultural pluralism is felt anew when the composition of the population changes. The tension between nations and provinces resurfaces when the aspirations of one or more of them change. And so on.

Latent contradictions in society may be deliberately and systematically exploited by politicians or groups for their own purposes, or public authorities may unintentionally stir them up when they plan for change. Whatever the intention, incompatibilities are transformed into social tensions and political struggles. Such tensions will be socially destructive when they are exploited for purely electoral or partisan purposes.

The Meech Lake Accord brought to the surface several of the contradictions inherent in Canadian society. Although the surfacing of social contradictions and tensions is not necessarily damaging, it may be so frequent or intense that it destabilizes the social order, undermines the cohesion of society, or paralyses its capacity to act effectively as a collectivity. There is a limit to the amount of stress a society can manage at one time. Perhaps in the mid-1980s Canada had reached that stress limit.

A society's stress threshold is impossible to measure in any systematic way. But a vital function and responsibility of leadership is to make a judgment on that limit before introducing a major change. In the case of the accord, that judgment was lacking.

The Need for Institutional Flexibility

No solution will ever permanently take care of the tensions among the three principles of equality that are part of the Canadian historical heritage: the equality of individuals, of the provinces, and of the two main linguistic communities. No institutional arrangements will ever accommodate once and for all those groups that define themselves as nations and provinces, or linguistic dualism and ethnocultural pluralism. Nothing will ever fully reconcile the principle of formal political equality among the provinces and their actual inequality; the social and economic needs of the various regions; the modalities of self-government for native peoples in all parts of the country; the protection of individual rights and autonomy and the requirements of social, economic, and political organization, or the pursuit of social rights and the requirements of economic growth.

New arrangements must be *regularly* negotiated to allow for the continuous presence of contradictions and tensions, the recurrence of social change and technological innovation, the complexity of intergroup relations, and variations in regional circumstances. The resources available and the current constraints can also then be re-evaluated.

The purpose of a constitution is to provide an overall framework within which specific arrangements can be negotiated. It is not an appropriate tool for sociopolitical bargaining in a complex, heterogeneous, federal society. "Constitutionalizing" can easily become excessive: it can result in the accumulation of institutional rigidities that make it more, rather than less, difficult to deal with the contradictory requirements of different situations.

The Limits of Constitutions
as Problemsolving Instruments

The most serious criticism of the Meech Lake Accord was that
constitutional reform was being used as a problem-solving device.
Some argued that existing problems could be dealt with within
existing institutional arrangements, and that constitutional reform
was not needed at all.[13]

Another view was that Canada's political elites are obsessed
with the Constitution. Critics claimed that "constitutionalizing"
matters does not provide solutions to problems, and in fact may add
to the existing institutional rigidities that must be tackled when
dealing with new situations. Both views reflected skepticism about
the value of constitutions as problem-solving devices.

The Constitution cannot attempt to reconcile the irreconcilable
through logical, legal exercise. It must have a legitimating framework, and in Canada's heterogeneous society the process of legitimation itself needs to be diversified. Even when generally accepted
values are involved, the demands of individuals and groups —
economic, linguistic, regional, ethnocultural, aboriginal — cannot be
evaluated and legitimated by a single set of criteria whatever the
circumstances. The credibility of political authority, for example, is
based on somewhat different criteria from those that legitimate the
structure and exercise of authority in business organizations, or in
universities or hospitals.

The legitimacy of the social order in complex, highly differentiated societies perhaps needs to be "sectoral."[14] That is to say, the
application of general values and goals has to be legitimated not only
in terms of the values and goals themselves but also in terms of their
appropriateness in particular fields of activity or social contexts.

---

13 The arrangements negotiated between Quebec and Ottawa with regard to immigration several years *before* the Meech Lake proposal and shortly *after* its failure
   must have provided confirmation for those critics of the validity of their views.

14 See François Bourricaud, "Legitimacy and Legitimation," *Current Sociology* 35
   (1987): 57–68.

Otherwise, the policies and programs run the risk of being perceived as violating the very values they are meant to apply or some other important value.

The question of official languages illustrates the concept of sectoral legitimacy. The arrangements with regard to language cannot, for historical, demographic, and other reasons, be the same in all parts of the country, or even in all parts of some provinces. Policymakers have already recognized this reality: different arrangements already exist in different provinces and in different parts of some of the provinces. The debate over the wording of the accord on this matter indicates the impossibility of making statements in a constitution that meet the requirements of diverse social and political contexts. The debate over official bilingualism also illustrates how a general value needs to be applied differently in different contexts to be accepted as legitimate.

Sectoral legitimacy could also apply to native peoples, whose situation varies considerably from one part of the country to another. It also varies with different subgroups in the aboriginal population. Accommodations that may work in one context may not be legitimate in another.

The Constitution also needs to be stable. If it is subjected to regular rounds of negotiations, it ceases to be a constitution. If it becomes an object of regular political bargaining like any other object of policymaking, it will lose its nationbuilding potential. It will fall into the politics of interest, when it ought to transcend such concerns — especially in its symbolic dimension. By providing a stable overall framework within which practical problems can be addressed, the Constitution can also give credibility to the institutional system and contribute to social cohesion.

For a constitution to be stable does not mean that it is "written in stone" and should never be modified. But decisions to initiate constitutional changes must be based on rigorous criteria.[15]

---

15 Parts of the federal constitutional proposals in *Shaping Canada's Future Together* read as a program for an almost endless process of constitutional negotiations and changes or additions.

Chapter 5

What Did We Learn from the Meech Lake Process?

In the transformation of the consensus over the Meech Lake Accord into a major confrontation, clearly no single political actor or event was *the* determining factor. In fact, what characterizes the episode is an accumulation of mutually reinforcing influences into a spiral of misunderstanding and hostility.

Although they were all intertwined, it is possible to identify four kinds of processes in the evolution of events. One was the dynamic of symbolic action and conflict. It was noted that the investment of symbolic resources, like that of any other resources, entails the risk of failure and, more seriously, of bringing about the opposite of what was intended.

The symbolic affirmations in the accord entailed risks because they suggested a possible change in the existing sociocultural order and referred to a view of society that was questioned or rejected by a segment of the population. They were ambiguous, so that different meanings were infused into them. These meanings were defined by what public authorities said and did and by the events that followed, and evoked in the public consciousness memories of past conflicts and controversies.

A political dynamic helped transform the debate into a confrontation: a number of individuals and organized groups in the country used the accord as an opportunity for political action. They saw in it the potential for symbolic or power gains, for compelling authorities to deal with their own grievances, for reversing previous institutional changes, or, in the case of Quebec *indépendantistes*, to mobilize support for their cause.

Some were drawn into the political arena not only to pursue their interests but also in protest. They not only perceived the proposed changes as important but also resented the lack of an institutional channel for criticism and saw the strategy of minimum demands as arrogant. Suspicions were fueled by the ambiguity in parts of the proposal, suggesting to some a hidden agenda drawn by Ottawa and Quebec City. Authorities did not appear to have the matter under control and, worse, could not be entirely trusted — because public confidence in authorities was already low when the process began, because of the secrecy of the process, or because of the perceived influence of *indépendantistes* or ultranationalists. A residuum of past controversies added to this mistrust.

To the dynamics of symbolic conflict and political mobilization and protest was added the dynamic of polarization. Society divided into separate camps. Particular social divisions — linguistic, regional, ethnocultural — became dominant in the debate. Issues were examined not in terms of their relevance for society but purely in terms of their implications for one's own group.

Extreme views acquired respectability and were generalized to include the entire "other side." Diversity of opinion in the population and in the elites was ignored. Those who were "against us" counted, not those who were prepared to compromise. Gresham's Law of Conflict came into operation: the moderates were progressively silenced and driven out of the political arena.

Social polarization led to communication blocks among groups and regions of the country. The targets of political attention shifted from issues to individuals and groups. Political discourse became replete with accusations and expressions of suspicion and hostility. The use of emotionally loaded language, particularly by political authorities, contributed to polarization, as did the actions and statements of militants and extremists. Memories of past controversies as well as climate-creating events, particularly those related to language policies, also contributed to the process. Finally, a condition facilitating the polarization is the mutual ignorance of the linguistic, regional, and ethnic collectivities.

Finally, the accord brought some of the latent contradictions in Canadian society to the surface of political consciousness and onto the political agenda. For instance, the accord raised the question of the accommodation of the equality of individuals, of provinces, and of linguistic communities — equalities that have, in some degree, contradictory practical requirements. It brought to the surface the tension caused by the coexistence of nations and provinces in our society, as well as that caused by the coexistence of linguistic dualism and ethnocultural pluralism. The tension between centralization and decentralization and that between individual and collective rights also became part of the agenda.

Meech Lake's attempt to resolve such social contradictions through the Constitution inevitably generated conflict. This was so for three principal reasons. First, since the two-founding-nations dimension of Canadian social organization was seen as giving priority over others, processes of intergroup comparisons were set in motion and resulted in feelings of loss of status, inequity or envy. Second, some groups exploited the contradictions for their own political purposes and for the promotion of their own conception of what Canada should be. Third, in attempting to deal with these contradictions, certain values and interests — political, economic, regional, cultural — were partly sacrificed, and were perceived by the groups concerned to be sacrificed *once and for all.* They implied a distribution of opportunities and constraints that benefited some segments of the population, but disadvantaged others.

In Canada's heterogeneous society, the symbolic dimension of the Constitution should be minimized, particularly those symbolic statements that imply a differential allocation of status to different groups or segments of the society. To be perceived as fair and appropriate, such allocative statements must be socially balanced — something that is extremely difficult in a society that is not only diversified but is also experiencing significant social and institutional change.

The "distinct society" clause was the most controversial statement in the accord. It came to symbolize for many a two-founding-nations concept of the country and the possibility of an unfair distribution of power. As a result, it became a divisive rather than an integrative symbol. However, since the concept of Quebec as a distinct society is here to stay, at least three issues need to be dealt with. First, what special measures are required to maintain and nurture Quebec's distinctiveness? Second, to what extent is the state the main agent of cultural maintenance and development? Third, to the extent that state intervention is needed, should Quebec have the entirely responsibility or should it be shared with the federal government?

The analysis presented in this study also raised the importance of legitimating institutional changes. That authorities think such changes best for society is no longer sufficient to justify them. Changes must relate to generally accepted values and notions of social order, otherwise they will be perceived as arbitrary or, worse, as manipulations by groups that seek to increase their power and pursue their own interests.

It is also important to recognize that legality and legitimacy do not always go hand in hand. A perfectly legal venture may not be seen as legitimate, either because of its content or because of the way it is handled in practice. Thus, when the legitimacy of a proposed plan is seriously questioned, it should be dropped. Values, interests, and culturally determined meanings are sometimes much more important than legality.

The fact that policymaking and constitutionmaking can be used for political action suggests that the timing of policy initiatives is crucial to the quality of the debate. Managers of change must take past controversies and the existence of movements for social change into consideration.

Policymaking needs to be seen as a three-part process. The introduction of change can no longer be seen as exclusively the prerogative of political authorities. It also involves informal bargaining — largely through the media — among concerned social groups and the relationship between the authorities and their respective constituencies.

This analysis suggests that the language used in a debate, particularly by the political authorities themselves, influences its development. Language can easily turn the debate into a confrontation rather than a reasoned discussion.

Policymaking requires institutional flexibility and pragmatic solutions negotiated in relation to particular historical and socioeconomic contexts rather than formal, "constitutionalized" prescriptions. Rigid constitutional solutions make pragmatic negotiations difficult and, as a result, generate social tension and endanger the effective functioning of the institutional system. In short, the principle of flexibility points to the limits of constitutions as problem-solving devices.

As contradictions are inevitable in any complex, heterogeneous society, the legitimation of policies and programs must be sectoral. They must be founded on basic values, but they must also take into account the particularities of different institutional sectors and different sociohistorical contexts. Flexibility is needed to negotiate the practical arrangements that will accommodate and reconcile the many pieces of the Canadian kaleidoscope.

Bibliography

Bacharach, Samuel B., and Edward J. Lawler. *Power and Politics in Organizations*. San Francisco: Jossey-Bass, 1981.

Bourricaud, François. "Legitimacy and Legitimation," *Current Sociology* 35 (1987): 57–68.

Breton, Raymond. "Multiculturalism and Canadian Nation-Building." In Alan Cairns and Cynthia Williams, eds. *The Politics of Gender, Ethnicity and Language in Canada*. Toronto: University of Toronto Press, 1986.

———. "Policy Decisions and the Competition for Symbolic Resources." In Albert Breton et al., eds. *The Competitive State*. Dordrecht: Kluwer Academic Publishers, 1991.

———. "The Production and Allocation of Symbolic Resources: An Analysis of the Linguistic and Ethno-cultural Fields in Canada," *Canadian Review of Sociology and Anthropology* 21 (1984): 123–144.

Cairns, Alan C. *Disruptions: Constitutional Struggles from the Charter to Meech Lake*. Toronto: McClelland & Stewart, 1991.

Cameron, Norman, et al. *From East and West: Regional Views on Reconfederation*, The Canada Round 6. Toronto: C.D. Howe Institute, 1991.

Canada, *Shaping Canada's Future Together. Proposals*. Ottawa: Supply and Services Canada, 1991.

———. Citizen's Forum on Canada's Future [Spicer Commission]. *Report*. Ottawa, 1991.

———. Office of the Commissioner of Official Languages, Policy Analysis Branch. *An Analysis of Attitudes towards Official Languages Policy among Anglophones*. Ottawa, 1990.

Clapp, Orrin E. *The Collective Search for Identity*. New York: Rinehart & Winston, 1969.

Cohen, Andrew. *A Deal Undone: The Making and Breaking of the Meech Lake Accord*. Vancouver: Douglas & McIntyre, 1990.

Coleman, James S. *Community Conflict*. Glencoe, Ill.: Free Press, 1957.

Coser, Lewis A. "The Termination of Conflict," *Journal of Conflict Resolution* 5 (1961): 347–353.

Deutsch, Karl W. "Political Community and the North Atlantic Area." In *International Political Communities: An Anthology.* Garden City, N.Y.: Anchor Books, 1966.

Deutsch, Morton. "Conflicts: Productive and Destructive," *Journal of Social Issues* 25 (1969): 7–41.

Edelman, Murray. *Politics as Symbolic Action: Mass Arousal and Quiescence.* New York: Academic Press, 1971.

Franck, Thomas M., and Edward Weisband. *Verbal Strategies among the Superpowers.* New York: Oxford University Press, 1971.

Friedenberg, Edgar Z. *Deference to Authority: The Case of Canada.* White Plains, N.Y.: M.E. Sharpe, 1980.

Galt, George. "Can't Live with Them; Can't Live without Them," *Saturday Night*, June 1991.

Gamson, William A. "Rancorous Conflict in Community Politics," *American Sociological Review* 31 (1966): 71–80.

Geertz, Clifford. *The Interpretation of Cultures.* New York: Basic Books, 1973.

Gregg, Allan, and Michael Posner. *The Big Picture: What Canadians Think about Almost Anything.* Toronto: Macfarlane Walter & Ross, 1990.

Griswold, Wendy. "The Fabrication of Meaning: Literary Interpretation in the United States, Great Britain, and the West Indies," *American Journal of Sociology* 92 (1987): 1077–1117.

Guetzkow, Harold. "Isolation and Collaboration: A Partial Theory of Inter-Nation Relations," *Journal of Conflict Resolution* 1 (1957): 46–68.

Hagen, Everett E. *On the Theory of Social Change.* Homewood, Ill.: Dorsey Press, 1962.

Hirsch, Paul M. "From Ambushes to Golden Parachutes: Corporate Takeovers as an Instance of Cultural Framing and Institutional Integration," *American Journal of Sociology* 91 (1986): 800–837.

Kallen, Evelyn. "The Meech Lake Accord: Entrenching a Pecking Order of Minority Rights," *Canadian Public Policy* 14 (1988): S107–S120.

Kemper, Theodore D., and Randall Collins, "Dimensions of Micro-interaction," *American Journal of Sociology* 96 (1990): 32–68.

Lijphart, Arend. "Consociational Democracy," *World Politics* 21 (1969): 207–225.

McCartney, Patrick A. "An Examination of Federal and Provincial Government Sponsorship of Voluntary Associations in Canada." Queen's University, Kingston, Ont., M.A. thesis, 1990, Mimeographed.

Newman, Peter C. "The Closet Federalism of the Parti Québécois," *Maclean's*, December 30, 1991.

Nordlinger, Eric A. *Conflict Regulation in Divided Societies*. Cambridge, Mass.: Harvard University, Center for International Affairs, 1972.

Oberschall, Anthony. *Social Conflict and Social Movements*. Englewood Cliffs, N.J.: Prentice-Hall, 1973.

Pfeffer, Jeffrey. "Management as Symbolic Action: The Creation and maintenance of Organizational Paradigms," *Research in Organizational Behavior* 3 (1981): 1–52.

Quebec Liberal Party. Constitutional Committee. *A Quebec Free to Choose*. Quebec, January 28, 1991.

Schelling, Thomas. *The Strategy of Conflict*. Cambridge, Mass.: Harvard University Press, 1975.

Sniderman, Paul M., et al. "Political Culture and the Problem of Double Standards: Mass and Elite Attitudes toward Language Rights in the Canadian Charter of Rights and Freedoms," *Canadian Journal of Political Science* 22 (1989): 259–284.

"The Sociology of Legitimation," *Current Sociology* 35 (1987, special issue).

Thompson, Kenneth A. "Organizations as Constructors of Social Reality." In Graeme Salaman and Kenneth Thompson, eds. *Control and Ideology in Organizations*. Cambridge, Mass.: M.I.T. Press, 1980.

———. "Religious Organizations: The Cultural Perspective." In Graeme Salaman and Kenneth Thompson, eds. *People and Organizations*. New York: Open University Press, 1973.

Turner, Bryan S. "Outline of a Theory of Citizenship," *Sociology* 24 (1990): 189–217.

E. Kendall Cork
Corporation du Groupe La Laurentienne
Coscan Development Corporation
William J. Cosgrove
Co-Steel Inc.
Pierre Côté
The Counsel Corporation
J.G. Crean
Crédit Lyonnais Canada
Crestbrook Forest Industries Ltd.
John Crispo
Crown Life Insurance Company Limited
Hugh A. Curtis
Cyanamid Canada Inc.
Thomas P. d'Aquino
Deloitte & Touche
Desjardins, Ducharme
Desmarais Family Foundation
Robert Després
John H. Dickey
William A. Dimma
Iain St. C. Dobson
Dofasco Inc.
The Dominion of Canada General
    Insurance Company
Domtar Inc.
Donohue Inc.
Dow Chemical Canada Inc.
Du Pont Canada Inc.
Edper Investments Ltd.
The Empire Life Insurance Company
Encor Inc.
Energy & Chemical Workers Union
H.E. English
ENSIS Corporation
Ernst & Young
Falconbridge Limited
Ronald J. Farano, Q.C.
Field & Field Perraton Masuch
First Boston Canada
First Marathon Securities Limited
Aaron M. Fish
Fishery Products International Limited
Ford Motor Company of Canada, Limited
Formula Growth Limited
Four Seasons Hotels Limited
GSW Inc.

Gaz Métropolitain, Inc.
General Electric Canada Inc.
General Motors of Canada Limited
Gluskin Sheff + Associates Inc.
The Great-West Life Assurance Company
Morton Gross
Le Groupe Commerce, compagnie
    d'assurances
Le Groupe Secor Inc.
Groupe Sobeco Inc.
Gulf Canada Resources Limited
H. Anthony Hampson
Hawker Siddeley Canada Inc.
Hewlett-Packard (Canada) Ltd.
Home Oil Company Limited
Gordon Homer
Honeywell Limited
Hongkong Bank of Canada
Hydro-Québec
IBM Canada Ltd.
Imasco Limited
Imperial Oil Limited
Inco Limited
The Independent Petroleum Association
    of Canada
Inland Cement Limited
The Insurance Bureau of Canada
Interprovincial Pipe Line Company
The Investors Group
IPSCO Incorporated
Tsutomu Iwasaki
John A. Jacobson
Jarislowsky, Fraser & Company
Robert Johnstone
John Labatt Limited
LAC Minerals Ltd.
R.William Lawson
Jacques Lefebvre
David Lewis
Gérard Limoges
Daniel Lobb
London Life Insurance Company
Pierre Lortie
J.W. (Wes) MacAleer
McCallum Hill Companies
MacDonald, Dettwiler & Associates Ltd.
Robert M. MacIntosh

McKinsey & Company
Maclab Enterprises
James Maclaren Industries Inc.
Maclean-Hunter Limited
Charles McMillan
McMillan, Binch
MacMillan Bloedel Limited
William Mackness
Manufacturers Hanover Bank of Canada
The Manufacturers Life Insurance
    Company
Maple Leaf Foods Inc.
Georg Marais
Maritime Telegraph & Telephone
    Company, Limited
Marsh & McLennan Limited
The Mercantile and General Reinsurance
    Company of Canada
William M. Mercer Limited
Merck Frosst Canada Inc.
Ronald H. Meredith-Jones
Miles Canada Inc.
Les Minoteries Ogilvie Ltée.
Robert Mitchell Inc.
Mitsui & Co. (Canada) Ltd.
The Molson Companies Limited
Monsanto Canada Inc.
Montréal Trust Company of Canada
Moore Corporation Limited
The Mutual Life Assurance Company of
    Canada
NCR Canada Ltd.
National Westminster Bank of Canada
Nesbitt Thomson Deacon
Noranda Forest Inc.
Noranda Inc.
North American Life Assurance Company
North Canadian Oils Limited
Northern Telecom Limited
Northwood Pulp and Timber Limited
NOVA Corporation of Alberta
Ontario Hydro
The Oshawa Group Limited
PanCanadian Petroleum Limited
Peat Marwick Thorne
Lucie Pépin
Petro-Canada Inc.
Les Placements T.A.L. Ltée.

Placer Dome Inc.
David A. Potts
Power Corporation of Canada
Pratt & Whitney Canada Inc.
Price Waterhouse & Co.
J. Robert S. Prichard
Procor Limited
ProGas Limited
Provigo Inc.
Quebec and Ontario Paper Company
    Limited
RBC Dominion Securities Inc.
Redpath Industries Limited
Simon S. Reisman
Henri Remmer
Retail Council of Canada
Grant L. Reuber
R.T. Riley
Robin Hood Multifoods Inc.
Rogers Communications Inc.
Rothschild Canada Inc.
The Royal Bank of Canada
Royal Insurance Company of Canada
Royal Trust
St. Lawrence Cement Inc.
Sandwell Inc.
Saskoil
Guylaine Saucier
André Saumier
The Hon. Maurice Sauvé
Sceptre Investment Counsel
Sceptre Resources Limited
Dick Schmeelk
ScotiaMcLeod Inc.
Sears Canada Inc.
Sharwood and Company
Shell Canada Limited
Sherritt Gordon Limited
Sidbec-Dosco Inc.
Le Soleil
Southam Inc.
Derek J. Speirs
Philip Spencer, Q.C.
Standard Life Assurance Company
Stikeman, Elliott, Advocates
Strategico Inc.
Sun Life Assurance Company of Canada

Suncor Inc.
Swiss Bank Corporation (Canada)
Teck Corporation
Laurent Thibault
3M Canada Inc.
The Toronto Dominion Bank
Toronto Star Newspaper Limited
The Toronto Stock Exchange
TransAlta Utilities Corporation
TransCanada PipeLines Limited
Trimac
Trizec Corporation Ltd.
Robert J. Turner

Unilever Canada Inc.
Urgel Bourgie Limitée
Manon Vennat
VIA Rail Canada Inc.
J.H. Warren
West Fraser Timber Co. Ltd.
Westcoast Energy Inc.
George Weston Limited
Alfred G. Wirth
M.K. Wong & Associates Ltd.
Wood Gundy Limited
Xerox Canada Inc.
Zurich Life Insurance of Canada

Honorary Members

G. Arnold Hart
David Kirk
Paul H. Leman

A.M. Runciman
J. Ross Tolmie, Q.C.